In Search for *Love* and **Freedom:**

what I lost on my way...

Dr. LaShonda B. Fuller

Copyright © 2014 Dr. LaShonda B. Fuller
All rights reserved.
ISBN-10: 0990958809
ISBN-13: 978-0-9909588-0-2

DEDICATION

Na'Tasha, Briana, William, Amari, T'Keyia, my unborn children, and those who God has blessed me to Mother, I dedicate this book to you. As you tread your personal journey of exploring life and how your identity should impact the world around you, I can only hope that your quiet time leads you down the trail less traveled. Make a huge impact, even if you have to stand exposed alone.

THE JOURNEY'S MAP

Acknowledgments   i
Forward   ii

Introduction   Pg. 1

The Journey Begins
1. Confessions Intro   Pg. 7
2. Retrace Your Steps   Pg. 11
3. Psychologically Damaged   Pg. 23

Looking For Something?
4. ...Security!   Pg. 35
5. ... An Identity!   Pg. 49
6. ...Stability!   Pg. 97

Love and Freedom
7. Lost on the Journey   Pg. 111
8. Found on the Path   Pg. 125
9. Confessions Outro   Pg. 135

ACKNOWLEDGMENTS

This project was inspired from a place of lost, a place of pain that at first sight, family was blamed. Thank you Mom & Dad for your incredible demonstration of survival and giving me all that you were able to give. Your story propelled my story. Pen, thank you for pushing me to SCRIBE even as I feared how others might be impacted by my reality. Nick and Melissa, great work on the cover! Your imagination captured the images I would like to leave my readers with, which is to remain focused on the promise, a rainbow amidst the clouds. And to all of my safe houses, I am indebted to your care.

FORWARD

"... I have always wondered how women exist amidst pain."
-Dr. LaShonda Fuller

The Journey Begins.

Carelessness is a big problem for many people. Misplacing things in a rush to do something else is a common behavior, yet can be an indicator of being internally unsettled if it happens frequently. Losing something of value monetarily is quite different than losing something that is priceless, but a lost thing can cause great distress depending upon what it means to the person who lost it. When we recognize the value of the things we possess we will not know how to, or why we should protect them from being lost.

Think of the woman in the Biblical parable of Luke 15 who lost one of her 10 gold coins. The illustration states that she sweeps the house carefully until she finds it and then called her friends so they could rejoice with her when it was located. Many people know the feeling of the peace of mind that sweeps over you when you lose something and find it again. But for some, lost things remain lost.

Looking for something?

A friend from college had a horrific experience of not knowing where her son was located for a week. Her son, the man-child, the King she was raising and pouring her love into was missing! You could live with losing one gold coin if you had ten but if you lost your child that would be completely different, right? Can you imagine what you would do if your child was lost?

Every day I prayed for her but I watched as she prayed for herself, giving herself life in the darkness of pain she was carrying. I was empowered by her courage and found a reason to hug my own child tightly before we left each other's presence. My friend's faith empowered people across the country and internationally. She never stopped holding out hope that she would find her son. In time, God brought him home and we all rejoiced with her in the testimony of his return.

The Lost and Found.

The depth of distress we feel when we lose our phone is not the same as losing a loved one or losing a special momento. Losing something that we can replace does not compare to things that can be substituted for what we carelessly misplaced or were taken from our possession. There is a difference, but lost things are still lost until we find them.

Dr. LaShonda Fuller is a brave woman. It takes courage to tell the truth and even more courage when those truths are personal. As I coached her through writing this book, it was observed how she battled with wondering how people would accept or reject her truths. In the end she chose to tell her story in spite of her desire for approval. If you need one, that is a great example of her bravery.

In this book, (part memoir, part workbook), Dr. Fuller exposes her internal and external search for two important values that shaped her existence: Love and Freedom. If you think about it, Love and Freedom shape all of us; there is no in between for either of these ideals. LaShonda has not only written herself a new road map, she has brought us along for the process so that we all may find true love and true freedom. As she exposed her own missteps, Dr. Fuller is teaching us what pitfalls to avoid and how to get back to our faith.

Because she is a licensed Doctoral level counselor, take full confidence that this author is offering a personal and a clinical foundation for you. Dig into her journal entries, read her poems, find yourself in the reflections and come out on the other side ready to embrace life fully.

In our personal conversations Dr. LaShonda has challenged me to think about my paradigms and pushed me to break myself out of my comfortable boxes. In this, I have investigated my thoughts versus my feelings, pondered how my childhood fantasy world and silence was fundamental to my perspective of myself and those around me. At one point I found myself reflecting on myself, my mother and my daughter and time stood still. This is how powerful reading this book was for me as her writing coach.

Do not ever stop looking for what you have lost, don't give up hope that God will restore you. You must identify your support system and lean on them like they are tree trunks. God has a plan for all of us and even in the midst of our lost things, God teaches us that God is all that we need.

Thank you LaShonda for being an example to us all and for allowing me to walk this journey with you.

Penda L. James, M.Ed.

InSCRIBEd Inspiration, LLC
Writing Coach

INTRODUCTION

When people are in search for something they have lost, they immediately begin to retrace their steps. I try to walk my most recent path until my present moment in attempt to discover the very thing I lost. This experience can be very anxiety provoking for me depending on the meaningfulness of what I lost.

I once lost my purse, which held all of my credit cards and identification. My heart thumped a thousand miles per minute as I ruminated on the thought of my identity possibly being stolen. I asked myself aloud, *"Now how could you have misplaced your purse?"* I must have looked in my closet four times, peeked in the bathroom three times thinking, *"Now why would my purse be in the bathroom?"* I scanned the living room and the kitchen.

Then I thought, *"My purse is in the car! Thank God my car is in the garage!"* So I walked confidently to my car, trusting that my purse would be sitting on the front seat, only to find my front seat purse-less. I panicked! But I did not have time to continue searching; I had less than 30 minutes to get to work. In the process of my search and retracing my steps, within 20 minutes, I lost my peace of mind too. Behind my peace followed my trust in people. I thought, *"Wherever my purse is, someone has found it and… I need to cancel my credit cards…"* Before I knew it, I had a running "things to do list" in my head intended to protect my identity. Instantly, I became weary of all the steps I would have to take to rebuild my identity. Then I prayed.

It is much more complicated when you are in search for something and you have no idea where to look. Figuratively speaking, looking for something with no map is like blazing unchartered territories; you do not know what you will discover. Oftentimes, when people are trying to get to a new destination without a map, they stand the risk of running into dark valleys, dead end roads, or even one-way streets. I think it is safe to say being lost heightens one's anxiety and may possibly cause one to feel hurried to get back on a road *or* **the** road that can lead them to their destination.

Based on the cover of this book, you might already be imagining that the collected stories presented on the following pages are based on someone looking for romantic love and freedom from past mistakes. Or, you may presume that the stories illustrated depict how one finds love and freedom from a loveless life of imprisonment. You may even be wondering what was lost during the journey because no matter how short or long the trip, we always lose or leave something behind. I always leave something behind when I travel.

Many times I have left my toothbrush or my

necessity bag with my toothbrush inside, thinking that the bag was buried under my clothes in my suitcase. I have gone on trips with no underwear in my bag, simply because I was in a rush to get some place!

Are you in a rush? Have you been in a hurry to get to a specific place you think you should have been at in life or a place you believe your life should be currently? If so, what are some of the valuable items you have lost while trying to speed up time?

When people are rushing to get someplace they believe they should be in life, they forget things. Valuable things, important lessons learned, and the essence of waiting. Some of the important lessons we forget, me included, are values connected to our roots.

And our roots connect us to our identity. In some cases, many of us need to uproot unhealthy learned values and replant healthier belief systems in fresh soil. When we are constantly watching the clock, however, vital purging and necessary gardening often gets pushed back until it is time to create New Year's resolutions, which are recurring and are unattended throughout the year. Life happens, sudden events occur and we know how to become easily distracted with everyone and everything taking place around us.

***

Tori desired a love without chaos and would fixate on what she did not have as oppose to embracing what was in her reach. All of her life, she yearned for what she believed was a normal way of living. She yearned for a "normal functioning" family.

This lifestyle she imagined consisted of attending the same elementary, middle and high school with the same childhood friends she would grow to call her BFF's. But that was not Tori's story. She attended three different elementary schools and two different middle schools. Because of the constant moving around her mother's lifestyle engaged, Tori appeared quiet in school due to the hassle of having to make new friends every other year. She walked unchartered territories with each new school and proceeded with caution because she frowned upon the idea of not being liked by others. Most of her worries she contributed to Sabrina, her older sister, taunting her with the idea that "you gon' get into a lot of fights when you get in high school because of yo mouth!" Once Tori became acclimated to her environment, her citizenship grade on her report card always appeared as a RED THREE. During Tori's grade school days, three's for citizenship meant you talked too much. She had no restraint once comfortable.

Tori also thought that a normal family included a household where her mother and father lived together, happy. You know, like the Huxtables. But she would accept a household where her mother and her mother's boyfriend of seventeen years lived together.

Tori's story starts with riding her 10-speed bike up and down Abington Street in the summer heat. Twenty minutes past the flickering street lights of her curfew, Sabrina stood at the corner screaming, *"Toriiiiiiiiiiiiiii! COME HOME!"* She knew better. Jumping on her bike, she would race for the house to get a cold wet rag for her eyes, infected by the grass she had been laying in and the bushes she had run through while playing hide-go-seek. Until the age of seven, it was only Tori, her sister Sabrina, who was 16, and her mother who lived in the house together. It was the three of them for as long as she could remember. Her father made occasional visits, until her momma brought a new daddy home. Although Tori loved the new presence in the house, her Dad's presence (when he came around) was still strong enough to stop every movement of play; only for Tori to run and jump into her Daddy's arms. She did not notice his absence too much as a kid because she was always entertained at a friend's or a cousin's house for sleepovers.

Bouncing around from grade school to grade school, after the seventh move, she really wanted to graduate from Drew Middle School, even if that meant catching the Wyoming bus from Eight Mile Road to Chicago Avenue every morning. With such a stern determination to keep her same friends, her high school years were home for her; stability. She graduated from Mackenzie High School as the Valedictorian of her class and looked forward to a promising college experience. The thought of attending Bowling Green State University, where the cornstalks were tall in a rural small town, for a year or two and transferring to another school was the last thought she wanted to entertain.

A city girl in a small town caused for her first year of college to be dreadful but she'd vowed to stay until she received her first degree. The continual moving around from place to place during her childhood was a nuisance for her; and she was determined to have stability.

Stability. Tori believed certain physical moves in life would free her from her childhood, unstable, emotional angst. Yet, she only learned that her baggage from her roots traveled everywhere she traveled, transpiring into unfamiliar relationships. She believed she would find love before walking across the stage of college completion and therefore, have her ideal life, her ideal family.

If only she had discovered sooner that going away to college would not free her from the floating memories of her past, or burying herself into a romantic relationship would promise her a fantasy come true, escaping would not be so frustrating.

THE JOURNEY BEGINS
1 CONFESSIONS INTRO

I have no secrets. What is done in secrecy becomes unveiled in the end anyway, right? At least that's what the good Book says. You know, the Bible? That's my catchphrase. Sabrina, my older sister would always retort to my life's motto with, *"You never let your right hand know what your left hand is doing – and that's in the Bible too!"*

Well the scripture she's referring to is in Proverbs 29:11 New King James Version (NKJV) *"A fool vents all his feelings but a wise man holds them back"*; (King James Version) *"A fool uttereth all his mind: but a wise man keepeth it in till afterwards."* Well, I'm no fool and I'm not angry! Maybe perturb.

The scriptures I'm referring to is also in Proverbs, chapter 27, scripture 19, in the New Living Translation Version (NLT); *"As a face is reflected in water, so the heart reflects the real person."* Wait a minute! I'm not through proving my case…

Psalms 139:1, the NLT as well says, *"O Lord, you have examined my heart and know everything about me"*; therefore, what do I have to hide? Because I can be mordant with my comments, my response would always be, *"How come? Even if my left hand knew what my right hand was doing, my left hand can't control anything my right hand is doing unless my right hand allowed it. So it really doesn't matter if you know what cards I have in my hand or not, you can't play em."* I can be such an irritant with my words.

Let me further confirm my position, Jesus said in Luke 8:17 (NKJV) *"For nothing is secret that will not be revealed nor anything hidden that will not be known and come to light."* Jesus also stated in Luke 12:2-3 (NKJV) *"For there is nothing covered that will not be revealed nor hidden that will not be known. Therefore whatever you have spoken in the dark will be heard in the light…"*

Maybe Sabrina had a point after all. Recently, I learned that telling everyone everything may not be in my best interest. But Sabrina is private anyway, so what does she know?

After I started to share my plans of traveling, or plans to relocate my occupation, people seemed to only offer me emotional drainage. That is when I started to believe that my sister's motto was on to something. Listening to the naysayers' lack of excitement or criticism caused me discouragement.

I am an extrovert by nature; so any slight disagreement really stirs me but doesn't overcome me. Some of those of who I shared my stories with were obviously overjoyed for my new adventures while others seemed a bit disengaged. Most of the time, I felt alone from their disengagement. If I can't share my life with people I love, then who can I share my life with!?

I guess that's what I'm searching for. I started turning cold when I learned that everyone is not for me, not even my family. Needless to say, I may need to caution what my right hand shares. But not sharing my dreams, my plans, my life… is very uncomfortable because I enjoy sharing my dreams with people I care about and who I believe care about me. I am a transparent person. So here I am, unveiled.

What are some of your own confessions *or* thoughts you might need to confess aloud?

2 RETRACE YOUR STEPS

I was close to innocent that is not jaded, outside of close calls with high school boyfriends. Thank God to my benefit, I was always able to walk away with my pearls intact and not handed over to swine. I was trained to be tough and in it for my gain. I think we all come into this world initiated into our specialized Parent Boot Camp.

There are rules, and one way of thinking in order to get along with the system and eventually move out with your parent's blessings. That one way is the Head Parent in Charge (HPIC) way. In my case, the PIC was my mother and one of her main rules was "If you get pregnant, **YOU** (sic) taking care of that baby. I raised mine!"

In Momma's Boot Camp, Sabrina and I learned the importance of taking care of numero uno (self) first and to trust no man. Being self-reliant was extreme to Momma. I was confused because she was raised in a two-parent household. It just did not make sense to me. As a child, I listened to many of my Momma's rants.

Most nights her rants included loud music, alcohol, and sometimes a few of her suspicious friends. When she cried alone she ranted. I heard how angry she was with her father, who had physically abused her mother. I heard how disappointed she was with her brother, who apparently was never there to protect her (as one would hope a brother would), and her grotesque disdain for my father. In one breath she would cuss out her boyfriend, Bobby, then switch her self-involved conversations and go off on my Daddy, who had not been around in weeks, and wrap-up her rant by giving my uncle the blues for introducing her to Daddy in the first place. Mrs. Jekyll would have a brief timeout but only for Mrs. Hyde to have time to say, "But had it not been for Mr. B., I wouldn't have my Tori." My mother's roller coasters of emotional grief ranged from her paternal abandonment compounded with the rejection from her brother and a lack of commitment from my father resulted in a generalized negative belief toward all men. Her belief system of men consisted of screw men, but not in those exact words. Momma had a way with words that would slice a man down to finite pieces of his body parts. She was raw – all liquor and maybe a chaser while she listened to Simply Red and Lisa Stansfield on repeat. As a child, I always wondered "why is Momma so angry?" Her expressions needed no introduction and no further explanation.

During those moments watching my mother I

learned to be a good observer of body language. I watched for the best times to ask permission to go somewhere to escape from the gloom and doom. I knew the right times to ask if company could come over for my relief. I had to be very careful about how and when to defend myself when I was often accused of being sexually active. You see, Momma had Sabrina when she was 16. The fact that I was not sexually active made me angry or even more adamant to prove how wrong she was about me. Other times, I treaded lightly when taking up for Daddy in his absence. I was tired of her down talking him. If her experiences with him were as dreadful as she made them sound, she wouldn't have anything positive to say.

If I was not careful with my words, it was a close call to my face experiencing the palm of her hand. It was a skill to know when to safely and quietly stay out of her way to avoid any confrontation. The morning after her night full of emotional rants was either like walking on egg shells or having a freedom party. If our dialogue became thick enough where bruises were left as my remains, I definitely walked on egg shells because nine times out of 10, she did not remember or she believed my bruises were warranted. If I was having a freedom party, it was because her hot box was keeping her glued to her bed with a cold glass of kool-aid to chill the fire in her stomach; therefore, I got to leave. I did not believe in fighting the HPIC; I did believe in speaking up, always have. Sabrina on the other hand was no stranger to fighting. She had had her fair share of school fights; although, her plea has always been, "I was defending myself from being bullied!"

When I learned that the kids at her school talked about her acne, I felt guilty for talking about her acne at home and adding one more thing to what she had to deal with. I never really wanted to hurt her feelings I only wanted to spend more time with her and for her to want to spend time with me. Because she did not, I intentionally talked about her face because *my* feelings were hurt. Sabrina did not have a problem with swinging at Momma. Maybe she was that angry that Momma was the one she really wanted to fight. When I think about it, the two of them never really got along. While watching Sabrina fight everyone around her in defense for herself, even Momma, I vowed to never fight her or Momma. I saw how angry Momma became when she talked about what Sabrina would get into trouble doing. Sometimes, she had no words to describe how she felt. I never wanted to make Momma angry but I hated when Sabrina got chastised.

Many nights I wanted to escape the loud talking, cussing, and my mother accidentally spitting in my face during heated conversations. I would have left but I was too concerned about her safety so I would only threaten to leave with packed bags. I thought I could save her and protect our home from whomever she would be entertaining. Many nights I stayed in my room with my ear to the floor and I would write. That is when writing became my friend.

***

> ### *I use to **LOVE** Writing*
>
> *Writing came easy for me. What the eyes see, but the mouth doesn't tell can read for a mean story. It's all in honesty. It was something to do when I needed to escape from my dirty laundry. She listened to my inner thoughts that could cut deep if I wanted them to. She dried out the rain when my life was flooded with chaos, confusion, yet an unquestionable amount of pain.*
>
> *Writing was my friend. She constantly listened to my dreams. When she started to write back is when I knew our relationship would never end. She'd always be there and wait for me to return again. She guided me through the fights with the childhood opponents, when running away from home seemed like the brightest idea for the moment. She was there, through the heartbreaks with the high school boyfriends we both knew would eventually disappear.*
>
> *Writing was my best friend. She allowed me to speak my truth and she read all between my lines, especially when I felt lost and confused most times. I'm sorry Writing, I haven't spoken to you in a while. But I'm grateful that our friendship has always stood the test of time.*

I was a good trainee for the HPIC. I protected her just as I protected my father. I knew the good that was within her, I saw it as she took care of everyone besides herself. I felt the good within her as she cried "who's here for me?" I was there when she problem-solved our life circumstances in a matter of minutes. I concluded that she was doing the best she could with what she had. But what about doing the best with what God wanted to give her?

Mother's occupations have ranged from a nurse's aide, to a computer operator for the State of Michigan. She cleaned the home of a messy educator and was a bookkeeper for an auto parts store. She was a "queen" of all trades. From breaking down and rebuilding car motors, to carpentry work in our fixer upper homes that she and Bobby made livable for us. After Bobby lost his job with Ford Motor Company, where I heard he worked ever since his return from the military, he developed people's homes for income. Bobby was the man with his hands and everybody knew it. That is why Momma stayed so mad at him because he developed homes for income alright, low income close to no income. Momma hated that Bobby charged less than he was worth but he was not licensed. Bob did not care, as long as he was busy; away from Momma long enough to keep her from putting him out, and able to afford their drug of choice.

In training, I heard stories about how my grandfather beat my grandmother. My mother would go on and on about how he would bang her head against a porcelain bathroom sink, which eventually developed the brain tumor that took my grandmother away from my mother when she was seven. My sister and I would never be graced with my grandmother's smile. It feels awkward calling him Grandfather because I don't know him. On weekends, my mother's father brought women home to eat dinner with his family after gambling and getting drunk.

I understand that this is not my story to tell, but the fact that I experienced the repeated telling of the story **is** a part of my truth untold. Momma would drink with her head hanging and sorrow welling in her voice from the anger she held so tightly in her throat against her father who had also deserted her at the age of 17. As a young woman, I never realized how the memory of my mother's sorrow and bitterness toward men would connect with my inner being and determine how I would see myself and how I would relate to men.

Through my mother's examples of pain and perseverance, I learned how to be tough. The training process was intense nonetheless. I learned how to aim and fire with words that would cause a person to bleed before they knew they were hit. I learned how to be suspicious of all people and their motives, even the HPIC. I also learned very early that God had me. I really did not know what that meant emotionally. Because I heard Momma said it all of the time, I believed that to some degree it was true.

Though I watched my mother experience rapid fire trials, I began to discover that in the end, everything always turned out just fine, just like the fixer upper's we lived in. If the car broke down, Momma popped the hood, tapped the battery a few times, maybe added water to the radiator reservoir and the car would crank and move. If we had to move, Momma looked for the next fixer upper for us to live in around the Westside of Detroit and ***literally*** turned the house into a home. She was definitely a survivor, and as a kid, my hero. What a life to recognize and honor.

One could only imagine how a woman in her mid-thirties experiencing the constant "hustle and bustle" with two daughters viewed life. In her Boot Camp training, she was left alone to fight off villains attacking her from the back, whispering in her ear with temptation that would change the rest of her life and deter her from her dream, whatever that was. As she looked for people who could be trusted with her left and right hand secrets and men who she could trust with her heart, she discovered that did not exist in her world – not in man anyway. No wonder Sabrina was so adamant about her privacy. She seen how Momma juggled men; yet this paradigm influenced both of us and eventually how I would view the world when I left home for college.

As a kid, I could care less about what or who Momma juggled. The heart of the matter was that I did not want to be separated from her. After the several moves, there were a few times when I had to live with relatives until Momma regained her stability to care for us as before. When we reunited, I was in fifth grade and I told her, "I don't care where you have to go, I wanna go with you." After the loss of the first house we lived in when it was only me, Sabrina, and Momma, my address should have been a PO Box number. Living with relatives never amounts to living with your parents. Living within someone else's space will never be equivalent to having your own space. Living amongst other homeless families within quarters where the lights shut off at 10pm, will always be the memory that propelled me into Momma's arms at night and attached us through what seemed to be constant hardships.

The enmeshed attachment we shared started to become disengaged upon the kid getting older and fed up with the same dysfunctional routines where the tune never changed. This time, my future called out my name for change. Though it seemed like Momma was trying to hold onto me for her own selfish needs, she continued to survive many unfortunate circumstances when I went away for college. It tore me to pieces but I had to keep living for me. Our relationship and our family dynamics changed as a result and never seemed to find harmony again. The routines of rants and emotional roller coasters followed me to college when she phoned my dorm room shouting through the phone, "You think you better than me? I'll take that scholarship from you and make you come home!" I learned that I had to protect myself from her.

My yearning for supportive and nurturing relationships may have had something to do with being trained in a household where my mother was emotionally disturbed. I searched for another to protect me even though Momma always said, "I'll kill a brick over mine and a brick ain't even living." She definitely trained me in the name of protection and possibly violence. But my heart desired a change. I believed college had something to offer me that I did not have. The way Momma viewed the world was not the lens I wanted to view the world through. How could I deny my roots that made me who I am? I cannot.

    I had to unlearn some of my mother's paradigms that had a strong influence in my world. Of course, I did not have to share her same experiences. Though Momma had sworn she would never let anyone physically hurt me or Sabrina, she failed to acknowledge that in her vow to protect us, she was actually committing most of the pain in our lives. Emotionally, Sabrina and I had become just as unbalanced as Momma but functional. We were able to see the dysfunction in everyone else but ourselves. As Sabrina brought children into the world and created her own family unit, she excluded Momma from her family dynamics, emotionally. I left for college. Momma continued living in "fixer uppers"; and each of us traveled our own emotional journey separate from one another, cold and alone.

If you retraced your steps, what learned behaviors would you discover that made you feel

1. Safe?
2. Afraid?
3. Motivated?
4. Lost or confused?
5. Faithful?

_____
_____
_____
_____
_____
_____
_____
_____
_____

3 PSYCHOLOGICALLY DAMAGED

The psychological development of girls is said to begin at the onset of or after puberty. Women are aware that this stage is an important process for girls. The experiences of puberty shape how we view ourselves within our relationships with peers, siblings, parents, and authority figures. During the stage of puberty, women are also conscious that young girls experience similar patterns of negative mood swings but we don't talk about the separation girls experience from the world.[1]

You may have heard your Mother, Grandmother, or an Aunt say "She is going through the phase." Or you may have said something similar to the following statement yourself about your own sister, daughter or niece, "She started her period and now she always has something to say or she don't [sic] wanna be around nobody."

From an African American cultural perspective, I

believe we dismiss how crucial this "separation" phase of puberty is for us. As young girls, we are all of a sudden dealing with raging hormones and emotions. We don't understand why everybody suddenly makes us sick and why our male friends want to "play" in a different way. As adult women, we grapple with not understanding why we are yet, still dealing with a range of uncontrollable emotions from time to time. We are quite aware that it is our hormones and people still can get up under our skin.

Carol Gilligan, a professor at New York University known for her research on the development of adolescence and women believed that females in their adolescent years experience problems with attachment and detachment. She said puberty is the signal for when young girls remove themselves from being related to the "childhood world" (which has essentially come to an end when puberty comes knocking). The young girl enters into the world of "voice." In other words, when female's experience puberty, our voice represents womanhood; our desire to be noticed and respected and seen as a developing adult, which separates us from what we believe is childhood behavior,[10] silence or being quieted and unnoticed. With this concept in mind, I am reminded of the scriptural reference, "When I was a child, I spoke as a child, I understood as a child, I thought as a child; but when I became a [wo]man, I put away childish things" (1 Cor. 13:11, NKJV).

Gilligan argues that the problem sustaining girls' psychological face-off between childhood and womanhood during adolescent development is the loss of their voices. In some households, children are raised hearing things like, "speak when spoken to", "as long as I pay the bills, you have no say-so", and "go play while grown folks are talking." Now while I do not disagree with any of the statements, I do think that the way in which children are spoken to will be the way of speech they mimic. I mean, in my household and households I often visited I heard these very sayings and were expected to follow them. And I did. However, Gilligan explains that "silence contributes to the problems observed in adolescent girls [such as rebellion or lack of communication], particularly if these problems are seen to reflect a failure of engagement [or connection in relationships] rather than a failure of separation."[1, 10] When a young girl experiences disconnect in a relationship with a loved one, she begins relating, responding, and mentally living within a fictitious world.[2]

When I went away to college, I identified every older woman who demonstrated confidence, who was well-spoken, and nice as a motherly figure. In my fictitious world, they were my arms reach Claire Huxtable. The fictional world women live in comes from a desire to establish and maintain relationships with other females and genuine connections with other people.[12] If stress in the family is high, research says children suffer psychologically.[2] When parents are under stress, kids are shut out and rarely attended to. Hence, the many nights in my bedroom or the weekend sleepovers away from home. It is a side effect of children or teenagers who feel neglected, rejected, or abandoned that they may appear as back-talking, disrespectful, asserting their opinion with attitude, and involvement in unsafe exploratory behaviors, which can also very well be developmental behaviors. I believe however, during child puberty, whether the family is overwhelmed with stress or not, a child's identity is forming and needs to learn affirmative healthy boundaries. The primary source of learning how to relate to others within relationships is the family. To raise healthy psychological children, who will one day become healthy psychological adults, the family must foster the child's need for intimacy (security), love (affection), and assertion of voice (identity).

Imagine your household as a child. Did you feel safe? Did you feel loved? Were your dreams supported?

If there is no sense of safety, expressed love through affection, and support in family households from both parents, young girls begin to shift into a resilient or survival mode. They dissociate themselves from their environment and repress damaging experiences. They make up a safe world filled with love, smiles, and some form of functional communication. In *Communication, Sex, and Money*, Edwin Louis Cole says when women have become victims of emotional hurt they try to bury the experience in the back of their mind. They hope to never have to remember the experience again. Because the emotional hurt goes unattended, Cole insists that the pain becomes "stumbling blocks to the real intimacy, openness, and vulnerability of genuine love" and that "... you retain what you do not release."[4] In essence, baggage is carried with you throughout your developmental stages. This is how pain is passed from generation to generation. Cole specifically uses the word "sin." I thought of my mother and what she possibly could have been victimized by while growing up without her parents. What caused her to shift into survival mode? I cried out for her.

In the book, *Meeting at the Crossroads: Women's Psychology and Girls' Development*, Lyn Mikel Brown and Gilligan conducted a cross-cultural five year longitudinal study on the psychological development of 100 girls between the ages of seven and 18. They realized during the study that the problem for females is central to being reared in cultures led by men where the male needs are placed above the female needs. Their study revealed that forms of violation and violence has led females and continues to lead females to disappear from "the public world of history and culture" and live within their "private world of intimacy and love" for safety and security. [This reminds me of what my mother witnessed from her parents that would eventually transpire into her life. What I witnessed and transferred into my own experience is a result of her experiences.] This private fictitious world forces some females to compromise between their voice and relationships. In my grandmother's case, I believe she sacrificed her voice to keep her family together. My mother, I believe sacrificed relationships to make sure her voice was heard. When I think about myself in relationships and what I observed in Sabrina's marriage, I think we both struggled to find a happy medium-unsuccessfully.

Research has shown that females sacrifice their voice **and** relationships *for* relationships to fulfill their longing for basic human needs which includes having emotional communication and responsive relationships.[10, 11] I wanted relationships different from what I had seen or experienced. Brown and Gilligan listened to the young girls in their study talk about themselves, their relationships, their responses to conflicts and how they viewed conflict. They listened to the young girl's hopes and their fears and realized that these young girls were living in a world they knew was fictional as though it was real. I cried out for Sabrina.

According to William James[9] a pioneering psychologist who studied the pragmatic theory of truth, if what a person believes is useful to them, the beliefs are true for them. If what you believe is working for you, how can one begin to try to get you to see the concept any other way? I hated when Sabrina would say "Momma has always loved you more. She hated me and would say I wish I never had you." Why did Sabrina have to live this experience? Within her mind it became her reality. The belief was true to her and her experience was real but I did not see it. I just saw Momma angry. It is almost similar to having a friend in an unhealthy relationship. From the outside looking in, you can clearly see the dysfunction but it is almost nearly impossible to get her to see how damaging the relationship is to her well-being because she "believes" she is happy or at least, happiness will come. That is how I chose to see our family. That is how Sabrina chose to see her life outside of Momma.

This concept can only remain true until the individual discovers that her beliefs no longer work to fill the need adequately. When a person is always aiming for acceptance from people, your own mother, and the feeling of rejection or misunderstanding resounds loudly in your heart, it is no wonder "we" make up fairy tales. I cried out for myself.

As I read about the fantasy world some young girls experience, I recognized myself as a young girl AND my mother, who was also still carrying the same worries and burdens from her childhood. I was looking into a mirror that I wanted to smash! The point of my sharing the acclaimed theory is this: I believe we are all guilty of fantasizing when we strongly desire to fill voids in our lives. The untold truth: we know when we are not in reality but when role play has gone on for too long, reality becomes the fantasy.

Let's make one thing clear, fantasizing and dreaming are two different things. If you are a dreamer, I applaud you because you have aspirations. Here are a couple definitions to however consider:

❖ Dreams: a strongly desired goal or purpose (*The Online Merriam-Webster Dictionary* fourth definition). *Wikipedia* (cautiously referenced), dreams can be creative thoughts that occur to a person and give them a sense of inspiration.

❖ Fantasies: the power or process of creating especially unrealistic or improbable mental images in response to psychological need *(The Online Merriam-Webster Dictionary* fifth definition). *Wikipedia* offers an additional perspective defining fantasy as fiction that commonly uses magic (in our human capability this would be manipulation) or supernatural (prayer) phenomena as a primary plot element, theme, or setting, which takes place in imaginary worlds.

We can now distinguish between dreaming and fantasizing. We can determine hurtful versus encouraging based on Brown and Gilligan's research. Their research also discovered that the girls' in the study were not only experiencing psychological dissonance because they did not want to lose a connection with people they loved but, these girls were aware of the sacrifices they were making concerning their silence. They were aware that their silence was helping them maintain a form of emotional connection with people they loved or wanted to be loved by.

I remember while interning at Hillside Middle School, my counseling supervisor, who I now call Mom C. mentioned to me that she used to ask herself why it was so important to me to win the love of my family. When first hearing that statement, I immediately thought, *"Why would I try to win the love of my family when I already have it?"* But Mom C. was quite the counselor and had a knack for peeling a situation. Until this research landed in my lap, I was unable to understand her observation and inquiry.

Like me, the young girls in the study were unaware of and did not care what they were doing to themselves; the girls were oblivious to the fact that sacrificing their voices for love was damaging their self-efficacy and self-worth.

This research was so profound that all I could do was sit on my bed and hold my face. My hands filled with the tears of my pain, my sister's pain, and my mother's pain. I cried for the young girls I worked with in group counseling. I wept for young women whose paths I had crossed and swapped childhood stories. I mourned for the young girls and young women I would work with in the future because I know they are out there, searching for love and freedom. I sat in my bed reflecting on how my relationship with my mother and sister had experienced multiple breaks and how I struggled with what to do with these dysfunctional relationships and others in my adult life. When a relationship has not filled your love tank you could refuse to believe that there is a break in the connection. For example, when trust or reliability is severed, the break in the relationship becomes confusing when we want to believe the break is not happening or that love is absent. At this point, loyalty and attachment to people becomes conflicted and the psychological struggles and survival strategies are carried into female adulthood causing psychological resilience or resistance.[6, 12]

Have emotional hurts from your mother, sister, or a friend kept you from having healthy relationships with other women?

Are you burying hurtful experiences from your past deep in your heart that causes you to be emotionally all over the place? Are your present relationships constantly experiencing disconnection? Do you struggle to get it right? Are you giving too much or not enough of yourself to feel appreciated? Are you accepting garbage to prove your love to people you want to keep in your life? Are you suffocating from distrust and you want to be able to trust again?

I am going to stand in the gap for the women in your past, present, and future. Please forgive me. I am sorry for hurting you and causing you pain. I agree with Cole who said, it may take longer for some women to forgive because the wall of bitterness, regret, resentment, and hatred has been built over time. So with this in mind, let us pray.

> *Lord, I want to be whole and healed. Please soften my heart and help me to see my experiences as you would have me to see them. Give me your eyes Lord so I can walk in Godly forgiveness. I release _____ from my heart and forgive them for _____ and ask that you forgive me Lord for carrying hatred, bitterness, guilt, resentment and any other ungodly spirit in my heart. In Jesus name I ask these things. Amen.*

In this moment, what are you thinking? How do you feel?

LOOKING FOR SOMETHING?
4 ... SECURITY!

In middle school, I fought some boys I dreamed about others. I shared stories with my Dad about boys I liked, boys who liked me and gifts I received. I was always afraid to accept gifts from boys because Momma always said, "You bet not be accepting no gifts from no boys. All they want is something in return!" But one Christmas I thought, *"I could use this wrapped twenty dollar bill. Momma won't even know."*

    Daddy on the other hand didn't have a problem with me accepting gifts from boys. He was concerned about me waiting for love. I was always excited when Daddy picked me up from school – it didn't happen often. When it did, I always jumped up and down and screamed his name. On this particular day, I was excited about someone else. I told Daddy, Allison, my future husband, had become the sparkle in my eye.

    While I shared my fascination of this boy with him, the hairs on his skin must have stood straight up because Daddy interrupted my fantasy. "Baby, please promise me you'll wait until you get to college to meet your husband. A doctor or a lawyer or somebody who's interested in the same things you're interested in and going the same places you're going." I gave a typical Daddy's Girl response, "Ok Daddy." In my mind, I was convinced that he was already found. When I left for college, I was on a "mission for love." After my freshman year, I confronted my Dad about the zero prospects available that he made me promise to wait for. After my talk with my Dad, I sat down and had a serious conversation with God. I made notes of all the things I desired in a husband, which included everything I loved and did not like about my father. I asked God to add or subtract to the list as I prayed, "Your will is better than mine." It sounded good, but I really did not mean that when I prayed it; I was negotiating with God. I believed that the next guy I dated was going to be my husband. I thought I was ready to be someone's wife.

A year and a half passed with no dating prospect. I was just crushing with no movement. I was becoming bored with the same routine of dinner and a movie rental with my girls. I thought I needed some testosterone, which would make my dreams come true and solve all of my problems. I was not bright enough to understand that people and future "trips", I invested my time in during moments of boredom, would operate as a "filler" in my life. This illustrated that I was needy.

A filler is something, or someone I had become fixed on to avoid conscious or subconscious emotional hurts in need of healing. The summer after my freshman year, I studied abroad in Africa. The Mother Land with the red dirt, sweaty heat, and natural body odors gave me many facets to explore.

I observed the physical strength in women transporting babies on their backs and carrying baskets on their heads. Gaping eyes of children chasing our bus and galloping toward me in the middle of the market calling me "Queen" and "Sistah" for anything to give to them loaned me the feeling of need; but it was not enough. I did not have enough for all of them.

My time in Africa was filled with lasting life experiences. I returned from my trip and focused my energies toward seeing the world—I have always been told that when you stop looking, whatever it is you are looking for will soon find you. So I stopped looking for my husband for that moment and took heed to my home pastor's advice. When I returned home for weekends, I developed more of a spiritual conscience through attending Sunday services. During one of my trips home I attended a Sunday's message of Pastor Reginald Lane from Dunamis Outreach Ministries in Detroit. There were many times when Pastor Lane's messages stuck with me; however, this particular day he spoke directly to my core saying, "You need to treat yourself as a gift box and fill your box up with all things that will make you great to have as a mate."

For some, this might be learning how to cook, becoming a better communicator, keeping a clean home, valuing your health or whatever that makes you a better person. For me, it was becoming more spiritually grounded, culturally well-rounded, and educated. I always said I wanted to be able to bring something to the table that would impress my husband. Pastor went on to say, "When your mate finds you, you want them to be able to open their gift box in awe saying, "Lord, all this, for me?" That became my new focus.

***

Charlie came into my life my junior year of college. Charlie, (named after the women's cologne), had a scent that no soap could wash from my body. His body odor was glued to my nose hairs, inescapable. Because of my prayer list and my firm belief, "the next guy I date will be my husband," I believed he was it! Because of the growth in my spiritual consciousness and my desire to save my pearls until I was married, Sabrina was determined to play defense. She said Charlie was a counterfeit, which were false interpretations of love sent by the devil. I dared not to listen. My need to be "noticed" was now being met. This of course was long before I even knew I had a love language that Gary Chapman talks about in his book, *The Five Love Languages*. Maybe I should have been more careful of the words I spoke regarding Charlie being my husband.

My words eventually became my fantasy, which I was determined to make my experience. I did not care about what Sabrina thought. What could she say to me anyway, when she had a husband and still lived in fantasy world herself?

If you are totally unaware of what I am talking about when I refer to a "love language" and have never even heard of a love language, I urge you to take the *Love Language Quiz* to discover what you value within your relationships. The quiz may possibly assist you in understanding why your relationships may be experiencing perhaps some misunderstandings. Take a trip and explore the website:
http://www.5lovelanguages.com/profile/

***

As a little girl, I loved Sabrina. I always wanted to sleep in her bed. I played in her nail polish and stomped the springs out of her mattress by jumping up in down in her bed when she was not home. I hated however, watching her get into trouble with Momma. It was like watching a horror film for me. And then, I hated that Momma was angry with Sabrina and despised to hear her say she was selfish and a big liar. Sabrina was not selfish; only when she would not let me walk to the store with her and her friends. Other than that, Sabrina did my hair, dressed me up, and played with me. We played jacks, connect four, and we colored. She was my friend and I was hers when she had to stay in the house. She taught me how to count money on the floor in the middle of the hallway. She French braided my hair so tightly that my eyes would pull back to make me look Chinese, but I took it. She would scream "Tori!!! Stay out of my room!" and I didn't. Nine years was a big difference between the two of us but when I got to college, she and all the kids came to college too. Sabrina and the kids would visit campus and eat well off of my meal plan for the first two years of my college experience. I was longing for something special, something I could call my own though; so, I was not trying to hear what Sabrina was trying to say about my life.

My relationship with Charlie was different from any of my other relationships. I prayed for him. But I prayed for all of my boyfriends. I prayed for his family. I prayed that God would change him into what I wanted him to be. Yeah, I really lost my mind too hanging his prom picture over my dorm room's double long twin bed. Kissing the picture before I went to sleep at night was my clue that I had lost my head and heels too. I thought when I loved Allison that I had experienced what being in love felt like, as a teenager. Yet, this teen had now become a young lady and I was terribly mistaken. I had not even given up my pearls yet. Unbeknownst to me, Charlie was responding to my love language, which caused me to kick my shoes off and dive head first into him. I did not see the rock my head was bound to hit!

If I knew what my love language was sooner, maybe I could have protected myself from the unforeseen ditches in my journey with Charlie. What ditch was I headed for at twenty? I was looking to be saved just as Sabrina was in her marriage.

I mean, Charlie was no stranger to the game and definitely more sexually experienced than "Tori, the virgin." Growing up for me, those words seemed uncommon and tantamount simultaneously. I had to deal with Momma threatening to take me to my doctor to see if I was still a virgin. Or else. My relatives made fun of me because I appeared stiff and naïve about the inside jokes that slid over my head *because* I was a virgin. I am almost convinced that Charlie noticed the dichotomy I wore on my sleeve. I sometimes feel embarrassed to say Charlie was two years younger than me, an all-star athlete, who came with baggage like any other knuckle head. Yet, as street smart as I thought I was because of Mommy Dearest, I did not even see this fall coming. Had I known my love language was "quality time," I would have watched how much time I spent with Charlie. (Maybe not, who am I fooling?) The truth is, the more we know what fills our love tank the more we want to fill it with what we value. Charlie and I hung out for four years consistently and between constant break-ups, six more years on and off.

Our relationship felt like a marriage, so I performed what I thought were "wifely duties". I was already introduced to cohabitation so I affiliated myself with cohabitating, premature engagements, and eventually silencing my voice. We had fun traveling, playing games, arguing like cats and dogs, supporting one another, and turning right around and hurting one another. My mother once commented, "It's a legal marriage when you hit 10 years." To dispel this myth, if you never marry, you are <u>not</u> married.

Consider this though, Jesus told the Samaritan woman at the well in John 4:17 to go get her husband and come back, where she replied she was not married. Jesus then responded to her saying, she was right but that she had had five husbands and the man she was currently with was not her husband. Maybe I treated Charlie like my husband not just because I wanted him to be, but because *when you consummate a relationship with fornication you become married through soul ties. The relationship is just not blessed by God.*

Momma use to always say, "The amount of years it took for you to fall in love with Charlie will be the amount of years it will take for you to fall out of love with him." Suspiciously I responded to her, "Are you serious? I can't see myself ever falling out of love with him!" From the looks of our relationship, I was not looking forward to 10 years of my life being in a pickle because I was in the process of falling out of love. I was pretentious about moving on yet, mentally insisted on saving the relationship. The more I tried to control the relationship through planned schemas, the more I damaged me. I found myself in a whirlwind that spun extremely fast. I did not even see eight years pass me by.

Things – We – Do...

When we came into this world, we had no clue of the things we would possibly do.
Role playing, drive-bys, rehearsing words, weeping eyes; thinking of words to say, losing self-control, behaving in such a way that you never thought until the very moment the pain of loss took over.
The restraints of "I will never" became "I'll do whatever!"
Whatever it takes to gain what I gave up because of the hurt and confusion.
But, don't I matter too? I tell you, this love game is an illusion. That little man called pain influences me to become evil; you know what I'm saying...
But to defeat him, I have to keep on praying.

When we experience a loss, nothing really matters but the loss. At that time, I have always wondered how women exist amidst pain. I maintained positive regard and empathy for others around me and was able to accomplish business as usual on most days. But truth be told, I was not whole. I was emotionally confused and not always mentally present with him either. I often wondered why he would treat me meagerly, offering me crumbs of a cookie. I prayed for him. I would wonder, *"What can I do to make him believe we're supposed to be together?"* I was afraid of loss. I did not want to lose him and his fondness of me nor did I want to lose what I could control, such as his need for me. I wanted him to be the support system I needed because I felt alone while pursuing my goals.

To keep Charlie near I held back what I thought was keeping him close to me. Eventually I held back my voice in attempt to get Charlie to run after me. My voice, the feistiness in me and my quick wittedness was silenced. I am not sure if I gave my voice away to save the relationship or if my voice was stolen from my vocal cords through manipulation when I called myself trying to protect him from his own insecurities and ill-preparedness to face his own fears. My silence connected me to my relationship with myself, my immediate family and my intimate partner. What was going on within me?

I began to follow the social and cultural encouraged pattern that I mocked and despised: this involved taking on other people's stresses while looking within myself to either protect or fix the broken relationship. I watched my mother bear the stress of a household while a man lived with us. I watched my mother get under the hood of a car to make the car run adequately so we could move from A to B, while a man lived with us. I watched my mother take money from a man whose eyes rolled over her body so we could have food in our refrigerator until the first of the month, while a man lived with us.

And now, the stress I watched my mother endure from another person's personal struggle, I carried into my own relationship. As a consequence, I struggled to maintain the connections that were important to me while my heart lay heavy from the disconnection within my relationships.[10]

Gilligan shared in her research that one of the best protections against psychological illness during a relational break or within a relationship where disconnection existed was a psychological safe house; a trusting relationship. A safe house allows people to safely speak freely, explore their inner voice, and be heard. Because I had hoped Charlie would be my safe house, I took myself through the ringer of psychological untruths, denial, and truths. I would ask God, "*WHY AM I NOT MARRIED ALREADY?!*" Then I would think quietly, "*If another chick sends me another invitation to another wedding or baby shower, Ima ... Ima go and be supportive because pssh...,*
I'm not jealous.
Lord, am I jealous?
Is Charlie really the one I will marry?
Should I or can I trust him?
Is he lying? No, I know he's lying. Yup, he lied!
Do I leave or stay?
How would I look to others if I stayed?
What does this mean about what I think of myself?
How do I make a different decision from the decisions my mother made?

> *How do I be me in my own process without the influences of my past, my sister, and follow the process that God will have me to follow?*
> *LORD, WHAT DO I DO???"*

I took Charlie through the ringer too. While grieving our "divorce" from the unlawful marriage, I psychologically moved from a phase of existing amongst my many questions to a phase of escaping them. During these moments my hobby became traveling and running from my daunting reality. What do you do when you're trying to escape your daunting reality? A very obvious reality outside of the truths that I was becoming so familiar with internally, was that my biological clock had "ticked and tocked." My ex was still my first and only lover and he was loving up on others. I was in graduate school where I constantly questioned my abilities because of my personal insecurities of competence. Either my family could not relate to what my life encompassed or they just really did not care because of their own dysfunctional and entangled spider webs!

All of the above placed me on a crazy, emotional, chaotic roller coaster ride. I struggled in my search for security. I was struggling and determined to get my spiritual relationship together. With all my many falls, my knees became bruised and had started to bleed. These out of wack emotions kept me busy. Ninety percent of my time was spent burning the midnight oil for studies or burning the oil in my car as I traveled Interstate-94 to get an emotional fix from Charlie.

The other 10% was devoted to burning oil in my head that often left me with tensed shoulders and a stiff neck, which is probably why I am in physical therapy now.

There is Hope in the Journey

Your trials and tribulations are only temporary.
Of course it depends on your decisions.
1st decision: Do you want a better situation?
Or are you comfortable with staying where you are?

2nd decision: Are you ready to experience another situation?
Or do you believe the grass is not greener on the other side?
If you answered yes to the first and third questions, there is no problem for you to move in the direction of your desires.
But what about fear?
Fear of the unknown. Fear of leaving what is familiar.
Fear of what a new journey has to offer you because you are familiar with the route you have traveled a million times.

To remove fear, you have to first identify fear, call it by name, and rebuke it; in other words, dismiss its' beak!

Then fill the place where fear resided with what you hope for in your journey ahead. Identify it and call it by name too.
PEACE! LOVE! JOY! FORGIVENNESS!
If you want a better situation and you believe the only thing in your way is fear, you have already activated your HOPE.

> I would encourage you to look in the mirror and tell fear, "I AM NOT AFRAID OF YOU!" It may sound contradictory but it is not. It may seem crazy, and yes, it is. Yes, cry. Let it out. Feel the tears as they roll down your face. Taste the salt in your tears. They are releasing the pain you've clutched so tightly in your palm as if to protect it.
>
> But sometimes not even this is helpful, if the fall in fear is deep.

After you have discovered your love language, how will you effectively communicate your needs in your valued relationships?

_____
_____
_____
_____
_____
_____
_____
_____

5 ... AN IDENTITY!

I often think of the analogy Pastor Joel Brooks of Christian Life Center in Kalamazoo, Michigan gives in his book co-authored with Michelle McKinney-Hammond, *The Unspoken Rules of Love: What Women Don't Know and Men Don't Tell* about shopping around in relationships. I understand the quest behind shopping for something and hoping for a particular inexpensive item.

Think about it for a minute, who does not like a good deal? If you are anything like me, you go into a store and head straight for the clearance section. You will not stop until you have saved more than a few dollars. When you come across an item but the cost is more than what you agree to spend, do you think, *"Where can I get this item for cheaper?"*

According to Brooks and Hammond, we look around the store to see if we can find something *similar* to what we *really want* that is not as costly; essentially, we settle. When you think about it, *when* you buy the cheaper item, are you ever really satisfied with your purchase? I don't think so. If you are anything like me, you wonder how you can get the actual item you wanted, and the other item. Brooks and Hammond used this metaphor to describe men who are not ready for marriage and how they shop around for women who are willing to satisfy their immediate needs. I believe this concept also pertains to women who are shopping around for emotional fixes. We entertain the idea that something may not be fulfilling but may do until we spot the right, or perfect buy. But wait a minute! What exactly are we looking to buy? I'll tell you, *an identity*.

Arizona

Outside of driving up and down Interstate-94 to meet up with Charlie, I was in an airplane cheating on depression with adventure. My first escape started when I met "Nice Guy" in Arizona. Nice Guy did not last long because I was only really shopping around. I knew exactly what I was looking for and Nice Guy was not it. I was looking for my self-worth, which I lost somewhere on I-94. The 2007 NBA All-Star weekend in Arizona created memories that would begin an ongoing need for self-reflection.

That year I created my bucket list. It started with paying $100 to get into a club. Honestly, I wasn't that interested in getting into *that* club *that* badly *that* night. I believed the distraction would calm the woes from the drama and agony of my stringy relationship with Charlie. There were quite a few celebrities in the house, so I entertained the idea that I was amongst the best of em'. Nikki spotted Kevin Hart sitting in a booth but I did not know who he was. Nikki knew where all the celebrities were posted. She had walked around the place several times. I sat at the bar the entire night sipping; I don't aspire to the groupie mentality.

***

Nikki is my older niece who can sometimes appear awestruck by fame. I promised her a trip somewhere if she showed me a good report card. In her second year of college, she began dreading school. Because she had always looked up to me and admired my lifestyle of staying on the go, I figured if I lured her to stay focused with a mini excursion somewhere where she could feel inspired, she would focus her energies toward finding the good in school instead of dwelling on reasons to leave. Come to think about it, I never saw her report card. I was just thankful that while I was still shopping for myself, I could afford an extra flight because she was definitely shopping too. But how do you model what you do not have? I needed this get-a-way for some inspiration myself. And the fun that came with it! That weekend I learned what hanging out with no sleep really felt like… exhausting! I had never done anything like that before in all of my years as a teenager *or* college student. Was I entering into an early midlife crisis in my late 20's? I hoped not. I was playing for the first time. Every night Ivy, Nikki, and I hit a different scene. While I was sleep in the back seat, longing for my comfort food, the bed, a good ole movie, and some homemade chocolate chip cookies the two of them was focused on our next stop.

"Is this acceptable while trying to live for God?" I wondered.

In high school, my friends called me the *"Mother"* of the group. My Dad calls me the *"Judge."* My Mother believes *"I think I'm better"* than others. My cousins, nieces, and nephew call me *"lame."* Go figure. Each of these characteristics has in common, calculated decisions if you ask me. What kind of decisions was I now making?

***

Ivy is my younger cousin who, I like to think encourages my alter ego. She's five years my junior so her style may be a little more modern than mine. Comparatively, she is Samantha in "Sex in the City." Bold, seductive, unafraid of confrontation, and highly protective of her family and friends. Ivy is one to have on your team. I fit more with Carrie from the group. Carrie is a little more reserved, loves a chase and excitement. Sometimes I can get too close when playing with fire and stay too long in a relationship. Ivy on the other hand plays with fire and runs from commitment. When her mind is in the right place, she can be open to reason. If her heart is emotionally conflicted, one should take notice and step back. Provide her with space and allow her time to come up for air on her own time; then embrace her. That's how we get along.

There was no way the two of them would allow me to stay home and be a glutton. On the last night in Arizona, I actually sparked up a conversation with a guy long enough to keep Charlie out of my head. He talked about himself and his bike all night. (Hey, it was better than looking for a place to sit in the crowded lounge alone). I listened, and ended up going on a date with him the next day on his Harley. Never have I ever, gone on a date with a man I met the night before in a club where a woman wearing fishnet leggings with no underwear casually pranced her body around for display. Yeah, I didn't used to be like this. I didn't always visit such places and if the rapture came that night, at that point in my walk with God, I would have thought that God would not have swung by to pick me up. However, I now know that those who have declared Christ as Lord and Savior and trust in His return, will be picked up! I used to be a good girl; close to wholesome (that being innocent), if you disregard the potty mouth. In my unsheltered world from the streets of Detroit, I realized I was sheltered a tad bit. Or, I was just disciplined and calculated most of my decisions, as I like to think.

There I was in Arizona, on a date with "Nice Guy", lost on the highway on a motorcycle looking for LoLo's Chicken and Waffles on Valentine's Day. With my eyes slit from the wind, using his back as a shield, I panicked and prayed, *"Lord, please protect me."* I was scared out of my brains yet, holding on like a pro, determined to see Wesley, my girl from back home, who worked at LoLo's. I had not seen her in years.

Nice Guy and I finally found this interesting building or house looking store front that was known for its' good food and where celebrities hung when visiting Tempe. Wesley and I screamed, "Hey Gurl!!!" at the same time.

***

Wesley became my girl, right when I was entering into high school. Sabrina and one of her older sisters, Tracy, were friends. She came from a family of 14, seven girls and seven boys. Her younger brother Lewis is my age and a chocolate cutie, who use to have a crush on me. I would be lying if I said I never thought of dating him. We had our moments of talking on the phone in high school but our relationship never extended pass his freshmen homecoming dance.

Lewis would jokingly say I was going to be his wife. What if we *had* dated? Could I have saved Lewis from becoming *gay*? I think it is natural for women to think we have a powerful influence over a man, look at Adam and Eve. When I received the news that he came out to his family, my heart broke.

"Thank God we did not date", I thought. His decision to be gay would have impacted my thoughts about my own identity in some strange way that I was not, at the time, mindful to process. I still struggle to understand how people can experience God and His greatness, yet remove ourselves from God and His promise, including me.

Regardless of what the restaurant looked like, the food was "the bomb". Nice Guy said he tried going again after our date and it never tasted as good as the first time. My condolences. To keep myself from becoming emotionally attached, I started giving guys nicknames based on my experiences with them. I described my thoughts about them, which reminded me of why I was not interested. I guess instead of calling him Nice Guy, I should have named him "Lanky". He was tall, had a bald head, a caramel complexion, and was a technical conversationalist (he was boring). Nice Guy was an engineer whose work revolved around programming computer software systems. I was fascinated by his travels to Israel for work. I was not thrilled with talking about computers. Like me, Nice Guy wanted to be married; however, he was married for a very short time. From his marriage, he left his teenage daughter who lived with her mother, and he rarely saw. From my understanding, they did not get along and he was trying to maintain a good relationship with his daughter as best as he knew how. This was too much for me! The oil started churning and I was prepping for my escape.

I know what you are thinking. No, I do not want to date a Mean Guy. But our date was just *nice* and it takes more than just niceness to engage my attention. Our conversation on the date was limited due to the wind. However, when I returned home, we talked on the phone for approximately two months. He came to visit once while he was visiting his family in Indiana, and we had another *nice* second date. At the end of the date, there was no kiss, not even a tight hug. His breath was not right and neither was my heart. Weeks later, during one of our nightly phone conversations where he was slightly intoxicated he firmly inquired, "You don't like me like I like you, do you? Would you be willing to move here?"

"What?"

Oh no, I thought. *I did not want to hurt this nice man's feelings. What do I say other than, "No, I do not like you like you like me. I enjoy knowing that you exist for my selfish reasons when I'm lonely and suffering from rejection from Charlie... who by the way is too far up his own butt because his new job pays great money and chicks are stroking his ego... which by the way is fabricated self-confidence."* No. I could not have told the blatant truth, *"I'm still in love with a knuckle head who I know is not good for me and therefore, I really don't see us having anything because I'm blinded, by your breath."* So I simply replied, "No, I'm sorry. But you're a really *"nice guy"*. Needless to say, Nice Guy fell off the wagon and his conversations consisted of talk about himself and his job. I knew I was still shopping around but I also discovered that I faced the reality that my heart had not released Charlie.

I suppose I was shopping until Charlie was ready to take me off of lay-a-way. With each new adventure, the experience became more risky. My aim was really to get over Charlie and to honestly, make him want to save me from my own self-destruction, if he had loved me at all. (I know, foolish thinking.)

I began viewing myself as desirable when Nice Guy showed interest. A false sense of value was saying to me in my ear, *"See, somebody wants you. You're not as bad as Charlie is making you out to be. It's him."* But, I was still in the midst of my sixth year of unwedded marriage. For the next two years, I went out of my way to date guys trying to remove the identity of "lame" and stuck on Charlie to an identity of "sexy." Yet, I burned rubber on I-94 and dug a deeper emotional hole for myself. Let's add another year to me getting over…

Muskegon

I was on my way to blazing a new trail two years later when I moved to my third city, starting my third professional job as a school counselor. In my case, all of my jobs were careers. I started months out of my Master's program as an Assistant Director of a Multicultural Center at a prominent university. I left there for greater opportunities. When I was finally putting my Master's degree to good use I ran into "Confusion." Confusion had a dual personality. Short, but athletically built, a conversationalist, but absent at times. He always smelled like a whisk of some "draw me nigh" cologne, not too much and not too little.

The scent of a man is tantalizing to me, which is why I was drawn to Charlie. While I worked as a school counselor, Confusion was, well I am not sure what he was actually qualified to do. I just know that I got to go to work and sniff a nice smelling man who smiled at me and offered non-stop compliments. We shared an office space so he always had a nice compliment waiting for my arrival in the mornings. I was always smiling during those mornings and going an extra mile in choosing my outfit, accessories, and perfume for that particular work day.

Most times when people lose a relationship that meant a great deal to them, they experience different phases of losing self. In my case, I lost the ability to feel pretty. I stopped investing in my appearance. While in my phase of investing time into my outer appearance, I needed help! Marge, my "roomie" and Tish, a colleague from my post-graduate program both had a way with heels. I had to be trained to mimic them. For the first time, I noticed how the shoes a woman wore accentuated her figure and popped her outfit. Me, well, I didn't use to be like this. I was a good girl, who wore comfortable clothes, no color nail polish – just on my toes, and no heels. I preferred flats and gym shoes, and oh no, definitely no make-up. I waited to get grown to "get grown."

The first time Confusion and I spoke was during a conference outside of work. We were standing at a pool table. I was impressed with his conversation but more attracted to how he allowed me to win our debates. I wondered if it had anything to do with those battling personalities we had in common, or the thrill of the mystery we both shared. I can be very competitive and he was too but I have to admit, I am okay with winning because of a stalemate. To me, allowing me to win says he is smitten, interested in something, or just trying to run game. How the conversation continues to flow will determine his motive. But I have found throughout my escapes, most men are patient and willing to play the game as long as it takes, just to see if they come out on top, literally! Well, I am embarrassed to say I lost my head. Yup, that self-confidence that I thought I lost somewhere back on I-94 was rising up again and fooled me. I think when women have gone through the ringer with trying to make a relationship work with one joker, it takes a minute to recuperate self-esteem and confidence (or a figment of it anyway).

    Somehow my conversations with Confusion traveled from work to home. After five months on the job, I decided to host a mixer at my house for the younger professionals. Confusion stayed after the party ended and we became more informed of each other. His conversation could go for hours with his penetrating stares that illuminated a sparkle in his eye. We talked about religion versus spirituality, purpose compared to mission in life, the kids we worked with, and ideas that would develop the school district we worked for into a more productive district. Conversations were stimulating. Confusion and I had poetry in common. Charlie was not really into my poetry. In my opinion, he acted as if he was just to keep me quiet. During conversations with Confusion, we would swap poems; then I discovered our poetry went something like this…

IT'S HARD… BUT IT'S EASY

It's <u>hard</u> to write poetry when I think of you because you, are so much like me.

It's <u>hard</u> to write poetry when I think of you and me because neither one of us, feel free.

It's <u>hard</u> to write poetry when I think of me and you because I become scared at the thought of what we could actually be – want to move forward but still, there's still so much for me to see.

It's <u>hard</u> to write poetry when I think about us because we're fighting against our emotions, encapsulated by words, behaviors, and stares amongst this lust; nothing else matters but those words, behaviors and stares… that encapsulates us, cause we're rooted from the same twin tree.

It's *easy* to write poetry when I think of you because your spirit entangles me and I just want to tango in the streets as our conversation crosses many beats.

It's *easy* to write poetry when I think of you and me because our communication is where we start, where we end, and where we possibly feel free to even begin.

It's *easy* to write poetry when I think of me and you…If I had my way and I knew this is where the buck stops, the worries, fears, insecurities, need for privacy, suspicion, past hurts, present concerns, and behold… a destined future, experiences would feel smooth upon thought, light over the heart, soft to your hands, and maybe allow us to just BE.

It's *easy* to write poetry when I think about us because you and I, well twin…, we get each other – but that's as far as we go.

Our conversations were enriching, engaging, relaxing, and kept me salivating but I wanted more. We eventually discussed a relationship between the two of us but I couldn't be too demanding. This man had three young girls and was just out of a relationship with the mother of two of his children! Besides, I was still shopping around myself and starting to get the hang of being noticed. GET ME OUTTA HERE! He was speaking my language, going back and forth with his ex as I was too. But hey, I was not interested in dating a man with kids, and THREE? No way! Quickly, I learned that although I requested stimulating conversation in the next guy, a man's conversation cannot be the only trait keeping him in the running. So I collected relationship qualifiers: a tantalizing scent, a nice guy, and stimulating conversations. I protected my heart and kept everything professional until my year was up and my transition was complete. Stimulating conversation is an important trait for me to have in any developing relationship, yet it is not the final qualifier. I do believe I started getting better at seeing the red flags.

Sabrina would always tell me, "Tori, never date someone you go to school with, work with, or who lives in your neighborhood." The truth is that if you do, your business is exposed. In the event that the relationship does not endure, you have to balance the dualism of the relationship. Well, I ignored all of her warnings … I went to school with Charlie, I worked with Confusion, and I lived within the same condo community as "Crazy." I should have listened to Sabrina!

***

Crazy was new in the district, an ex NFL player, and according to my sources, had no pension. He was persistent, displayed knowledge of the Bible, and *appeared* determined to live righteously. Crazy was a Christian man (my ultimate qualifier) from the South. He had one son, a passion for kids, and took care of his mother, which in my opinion, made him family-oriented. Crazy was also an entrepreneur and had a good work ethic. He had never been married but shared his desire to be married. What more could a girl be looking for? His time on the island lasted for two short weeks! The first week, he snagged my attention with his hook:

"Wow, this is *crazy*."

"What's *crazy*?"

"I feel like I'm sitting here talking to my wife", he said.

It utterly annoys me when people do not distinguish their feelings from their thoughts. For the record, when you say "I feel like" you should follow up with an emotion, a feeling and remove the "like", unless you are intending to express what you really think or believe. Allow me to show you using Crazy's example:

"Wow, this is crazy?"

"What's crazy?"

"I **feel anxious** (emotion), I **think I may be talking to my wife**" (his thought) or "Man, this **feels scary** (emotion). I **believe you're my wife**" (another thought).

My inside response: *"Whoa that is crazy. I don't even know you man..."* But instead I said, "Huh? Time will tell." And time sure did tell that his battery charger was insufficient.

His consistent pursuit started with calling and taking me out every day. I was floored. I don't think a man has ever been that persistent to pursue filling up my love tank. My primary love language is quality time; therefore, I am so with NOT BEING ALONE. I am a true extrovert, not just needy (at least at that time I wasn't). Well, Charlie was persistent in getting my attention too but he had something to prove. The guys in the locker room were convinced that I was not his type. I was a virgin who listened to *gospel tunes*. Was I a goal he aspired to conquer? Hmm.

Crazy on the other hand, was missing something that I did not have to give. The moment we had a misunderstanding, which led into him raising his voice, I stood my ground. "You need to calm down and quit raising your voice at me. It is not that serious." I had not silenced all of my voice. When he dismissed what I said by not even taking the time to hear my discomfort with his level of frustration, I hung up on him. First red flag: discomfort in a man raising his voice. After a similar misunderstanding, I told him, "I think we should just be friends. This is not working for me." Now, I had not forgotten who I was and what Parental Boot Camp training unit raised me. At no point was I about to allow him to disrespect me with his tone. He did not know who my Momma was! His response before hanging up on me was, "Well, fine then!"

And that is how Crazy got his name.

I remember standing in my bedroom doorway looking down at my phone asking Cayenne, my dog, "Did he just hang up on me?" and then I burst into laughter at Cayenne's cocked head expression. What grown man does not take the time to have a conversation and handle his frustration? *One who is not ready to have any of your time and be what you think he needs to be for **you**,* were my thoughts. As I reflect upon how Crazy was not deserving of my time after his aggressive fits, I pondered, "Why is Charlie deserving of my time?" He too, had moments of rage.

***

When the only grandfather I had ever known passed on January 17, 2010, the first person I wanted to reach for was Charlie. After the funeral, I went to my mother's house where I was restless because I wanted to be comforted and supported by him. Charlie and my grandfather got along. They would have conversations that annoyed me. Charlie would say things just to get my Granddad riled up and expressive as he waved his Captain Hook hand just so he could laugh at him. He mocked my Granddad's hand gestures mimicking his one finger and thumb on his right hand. The story I was told was that "he lost his other fingers in the Vietnam War." Did he?

Charlie enjoyed picking with people, especially my family members and then pinching my leg under the table to laugh about his childish intentions. Needless to say, I was happy he attended the funeral. But I had to reach out to him when he knew I had just experienced a loss. Why did I have to call and say, "What are you doing? Can you hold me right now?" Even though he responded, I questioned, "Why isn't he reaching out to me?" When he experienced his first lost during our relationship, I reached out by asking how I could help. I wanted to be there for him. He didn't respond how I would have wanted him to respond, you know, like *I* would have responded if it was me. Time, is not his love language as is mine. In fact, I used to always think his love language was affirmations. I don't know if time and affirmation mix well together. I would definitely become exhausted having to always affirm someone while spending time with them.

Soon after my grandfather's funeral I returned home and wallowed in loneliness. I constructed a plan to reel Charlie into my self-pity and back into my web of lust that was disguised as love. I called him, "Hey, I feel so alone right now. Can you come and stay with me tonight?"

"I have work in the morning. I'm sorry, maybe another time." Wow, that was too easy for him. It was in that moment I realized, he's gone… and I need to be gone too. At one time, it did not matter how far we were from one another.

We would meet halfway or one of us would drive the entire way only to have to get up extra early the next morning to make it to work on time. Rejection hit me again and another year was added to getting out of the self-dug hole. The only thing that called my name more than anything else to make me feel good or at least better for the moment was TRAVELING. Within a two year time span I had burned many dollars in the air. Miami for the New Year's, Puerto Rico for my birthday, Las Vegas for Spring break, and Jamaica for a quick get-a-way. With each trip came more fun and freedom depending on how you define freedom. Or, was it more bondage and risk attached to my identity?

Miami

For the first time in my life, I traveled alone to one of the busiest cities in America. Michael Baisden was hosting a New Year's celebration in Miami to raise money for the debut of his 'One Million Mentors Tour'. I was determined to attend and support. I was tired of bringing in the New Year hoping and praying that a new year would be different with me and Charlie. I was fed up with waiting for him to make *that* move and sweep me off of my feet. But what was I doing to draw him close to me besides living in the past?

The weekend's itinerary was full. I attended the evening events to preserve my daytime for relaxing. The first night featured Eric Robertson and other artists whose names are not ringing a bell right now in concert. I missed their show due to slow cab service.

When I arrived, I mingled and focused on finding a seat off to the side, where I could relax, bob my head to the beats, and analyze the words to the song, while I sipped my Shirley Temple. Mission accomplished. The second night was a little more adventurous. While waiting for my cab in the lobby before the comedy show, I watched a group of men unload a van. One guy approached me. "Are you visiting? What are you waiting for? Who are you in town with?" I don't ascribe to looking stupid even though I can agree to having made some stupid decisions, one being on this night. My response, "I'm here with a girlfriend."

"Where is she?"

"Upstairs visiting her boyfriend." I was apprehensive.

"Oh ok. Well I'm with Jagged Edge and we're in town to shoot a video. We're about to go have a few drinks. You or you and your friend should come hang out with us."

"I'm headed to a comedy show and she's with her boyfriend but thank you." As you can imagine, the conversation continued with him asking more of his prying questions. Did I have a post it on my face saying, "I am all alone and am trying to escape my daunting reality?" He eventually concluded our conversation, "Here's my number. If you get bored, call me." I was adamant about attending every event that I bought an expensive ticket to attend. I was not going to drop my plans for drinks with Jagged Edge and their side-kick. I did not care who was in town shooting a video.

I really expected to laugh until my stomach hurt. I think I was trying to make myself laugh with one of those gut wrenching ha ha ha's because I needed it so badly. The only thing I got was an "ahaaaa…" and an "ah ha ha…" I was totally disappointed.

He text me, "Are you bored yet?"
"Yes, I am!" After the show I caught a cab to the club where they were parlaying, as his VIP guest. The whole gang was sitting there sectioned off. I sat for a couple of hours, taking in the environment, the smoke, and the women crawling around with little self-respect, which I started asking myself, "what's different between me and them?" Just because I was not asking for attention through my body language, I did just catch a cab to an unfamiliar place, in an unfamiliar town, to see an unfamiliar man. You gotta be kidding me. This was too much for me. GET ME OUTTA HERE – and off in a cab was I headed back to my room safe and sound. I dodged a bullet that night that could have possibly caused more detriment to the self-worth I was searching for.

My time in Miami had not come to an end. I did not seem to use much more sense the next night. I was talking on the phone and exiting the cab for the New Year's Gala, when I noticed my dress was starting to unravel along the side seam. I panicked! Tish was laughing from the other end of the phone. I thought out loud. *"I know this fancy expensive hotel has a sewing kit at the front desk."*

I marched myself slyly up the stairs through the gathering crowds of finely dressed individuals to the front desk and said, "Excuse me Ma'am, can you locate me a sewing kit please? Thank you." I was **not** taking no for an answer from the attendant, so I waited. When she came toward me, I was grateful for the small package she passed to me. I ran to tack my red dress up in the ladies room. As I returned to the foyer of the hotel to get in line for the gala my heart started to relax from the racing my loose threads had created. After about 30 minutes of standing in line, an older woman approached me and said, "My cousin thinks that you are attractive and he is a really good catch. He has a good job and…" I politely asked, "How come he hasn't come over to tell me himself? What are y'all playing, shy cousin?"

She returned to convey my message of disinterest to him and not long after he made his way over to me. Nupe was from "home" in more ways than one. He attended a university 20 minutes from my Undergraduate Alma Mater. He told me, "I am very familiar with the campus. I attended numerous fraternity parties there." But I had not seen him. For whatever reason, I was miles away from home and connected with a fellow Detroiter. Strangely, I felt safe after my breach of security the night before. Nupe and I exchanged numbers and kept in contact for a month and half. Two intense dates after Miami, he began talking about a relationship.

"What are your plans with me?"

"I'd like to be in a relationship with you and eventually consider marriage."

This conversation took place after he agreed to review my financial plan, and provide me with the pay scale his company uses with their clients. There was no way that I was bringing myself to paying a man interested in dating me to plan my finances, even if he was a financial planner for ten years. I prepared my escape.

We planned to watch the Super Bowl at one of his comrade's homes the weekend of Valentines' Day. I did not want to send a misleading message of commitment or interest by attending this gathering. We were not serious. I could not get over the fact that he wanted to charge me to be my financial advisor while he enticed me with physical attention. I learned that mixing business with pleasure never works in relationships. I was not planning to marry Nupe. I was just starting to enjoy the feeling of being single. I escaped with a departing gift. To my surprise, he was not going down without a fight. How dare him not get the picture and want to convince me that this could work! My self-esteem tank was definitely increasing. My strength outside of Charlie was increasing too, or at least I thought. With each new male introduction, I started shedding the idea that Charlie was forever. With each new introduction, my self-reflection time was also increasing.

When I recounted my stories to Sabrina, she was bewildered about the things I did when traveling. "Who *are* you and where do you get the nerves to do the stuff that you do?" When I look back, I think about how naïve I must have seemed to people who listened to my spontaneous events. I thought I was tough, immortal, street smart, and could *protect* myself because I was trained in Mommy Dearest boot camp; I was exposing myself to vulnerable situations. I could have easily lost what was left of my heart and mind. And for what? Adventure? Attention? A new guy and an experience to talk about with my girls while I longed for true love? Who was I fooling? Just another event to take my mind away from the internal pain I faced when "it was me and my four walls." Before God would have me go into quiet time to re-evaluate myself, my identity, my goals, my values, **and** my next moves, I had one more stop to make. It was my 'Dirty Thirty!'

Puerto Rico

Some believe that when I hook up with Ivy, I get into trouble or make decisions that are out of my character. In reality, I have a ball being my alter ego. Ivy and I partied in Puerto Rico with her girls until we fell asleep and partied some more when we woke up. I wore sunglasses for the fear of someone seeing my glazed eyes. No one on the island knew me nor would they ever see me again. One night, there were two male visitors in our room, where seven women shared two beds.

There was no way they could have taken us all at once, I thought. But with toxins clouding one's judgment, who knew what could have happened. That night, a murder scene took place.

While the two men entertained a few of the ladies on our balcony, my paranoia led me to believe our life was in jeopardy. I tried to convince the others of my visions. No one listened to me but I was so afraid to leave them. I kept whispering to Ivy, "We gotta get out here" for her to only look at me with this blank stare. I was in a strange land surrounded by a foreign language and was so out of my comfort zone. I left the room for the sake of saving my own life. The others were on their own.

I woke up the next morning glad to be alive. The scene was all in my head. I kept thinking to myself, *I did **not** use to be like this. No! What happened to me?* It hit me – I needed a breakthrough. I was toiling mentally, emotionally and spiritually and was not sure where I was headed next. At that very moment, my spirit was weak but my will was stronger. I needed to tap into my vertical connection and I did not want to impact the others with my own conviction and self-reflection time. I decided to escape and take time to be with God. I woke up Sunday morning while everyone was sleeping and slipped away. I had breakfast with God and my Bible. There were some things I needed to share with Him that I was not too proud of. One was my trips for avoidance that only led me to the conclusion that I could not dodge myself any longer.

The second concern I needed to ask was "what was really going on within me" that I was not taking the time to look at and work on. I allowed myself to be distracted by the traveling, the blaming Charlie for my emotional angst, and my biological clock. The third topic I needed to discuss with God was this whole idea of turning 30. Surprisingly, turning 30 was scary for me. Turning 30 with no husband and no kids! Some people see this as an accomplishment; however, the idea of me being unmarried, made turning 30 even scarier. I was not sure what 30 should look like. I just knew it could not mirror my twenties, with a broken heart and no place to call home. I needed stability.

After breakfast, I walked the streets of Puerto Rico. I caught the bus to the marketplace where I took pictures of art and people, purchased gifts for the family, and a token for myself that I will always remember as my 30th birthday gift to me. While touring the town and peeping in and out different stores, I came across a jewelry store. At first, I was only looking but I needed something that would help me keep up with and respect time; something that would help me cherish each given moment. This would hopefully be a symbol of times changing in my life. I needed something I would be able to look at and say, "My, time sure does fly." It was time for me to start considering what I was doing with my time and how I must be intentional to use it wisely. "Sir, may I see this watch outlined in diamonds?"

"Which one?"

I pressed my index finger against the glass pointing to the sparkling silver time keeper and left a smudge on the counter. "How much is it? I'll take it." At that moment, time started to shift my perspective on my life and change my outlook on the years to come. My birthday was not long after I returned from Puerto Rico. Right before the milestone day, I pulled up to my apartment complex and sat in my car. I would sometimes sit in my car sunk down in my seat with my leg cocked up and knee against the steering wheel. My eyes closed, thoughts racing. I don't know why, but I would sit there and ponder before going into the house to greet Cayenne. One day I wondered aloud, *"What am I doing here? God, what should turning 30 look like for me?"*

"What do you think it should look like?" I heard him inquire. *I thought a 30 year old should look like a mature person who is comfortable with self. A 30 year old should be at a place in their life where situations and accusations are not taken personally. They don't let small things get to them and they're not settling for anything less than the best of what life has to offer.* I recall God saying to me, "Well, that's what you shall become." Later I also thought about how turning thirty would be different if I knew my purpose and operated in my gifts. I spent quality time with God on my birthday weekend to write a plan of action for my life. I was tired of being unhappy and stuck in the past. When I opened my journal to the top of the page the quote said:

> *Delight thyself also in the Lord, and he shall give thee the desires of thine heart* (Psalm 37:4)

The weekend brought this scripture alive for me in more ways than one. I arrived at the JW Marriott on the day of my birthday to a spread of fruit, cheese and crackers, rose petals across my bed, and a birthday card signed by the staff wishing me a "Happy 30th Birthday".

"Thank you Lord", I breathed a sigh of relief. The day of my thirtieth started with Cayenne, a breed of Pomeranian and Bison, waking me up as usual with excitement to go potty. Cayenne's my accountability partner. Her presence insists that I am not alone and that I take care of her. Her pawing at my leg gets me moving when I am not my best and dread detaching from my bed. Her excitement to see me when entering the door demands that I see the brighter side of the day when the day seems gloomy. Cayenne's expressions in many ways have made me laugh at myself. I wondered if she knew it was my birthday. Dressing for work that morning was fun and work was productive. My summer birthday is always at the end of the school year. There were several honor assemblies taking place this day and my attendance was expected. The work day was light. After work, my first softball game since high school was invigorating for a total body workout. I hit a foul ball and was super excited that I – hit – the – ball! After the game, I took Cayenne to Ms. Deb, who enjoyed Cayenne and her spunk so much that she kept her for me occasionally.

I believe it is true when they say dogs imitate their masters. Spunk I have; although people, who know Cayenne, say Cayenne is funny acting. Sometimes she was excited to see me and other times, she just wanted to relax in her own world and would not bother to move when I left. Was this me? Ms. Deb volunteered to keep Cayenne for the entire weekend so I could relax. The deep Jacuzzi tub in my room was calling my name for soaking. The next morning, God and I had a two hour date with a masseuse for a chocolate body wrap and massage. The day's journaling was led with the following scripture that I thought depicted the moment perfectly!

Pleasant words are as a honeycomb, sweet to the soul, and health to the bones
(Proverbs 16:24)

My conversation that day started with praises and thanksgiving to God for the moment.

"This morning, the chocolate body wraps and two hour massage was like a honeycomb, sweet to my body and health to my soul. Lord, the most amazing part was when I discovered that the massage therapist was playing instrumental Gospel music. "You are the air I breathe" and "Our God is an awesome God" were the melodies I identified [amongst some of her tunes], which made those two hours much more important and worthwhile. I worshipped – My body worshipped – You were there with me.

The salad and fruit was just right, after an exfoliating experience, and rest. The scripture you will have me to meditate on is Romans 10:3 - *For they don't understand God's way of making people right with himself. Refusing to accept God's way, they cling to their own way of getting right with God by trying to keep the law.*
My interpretation: "Whoever seeks to form their own righteousness does not submit to God's righteousness." Lord, today was filled with rest, peace, and an overwhelming feeling of joy. I long to hear your direction on the concerns of my heart, I surrender to you for your plan to be followed through. In Your Mighty name Jesus. Amen" 6/5

This was just what I needed. When we began to design my plan of action for my life, we discussed my inner/verbal dialogues.

- My appearance – I would like to lose 10lbs, laser my facial hairs, and have a flat stomach. I hate my toes because of the corns newly formed! [From the heels I insist on wearing in attempt to become more modern in my style]
- My work – Not sure exactly what I want to do because there is so much I'm interested in; I do not want to be a school counselor for long.
- My intelligence – Sometimes, the more education I achieve the slower I feel. My vocabulary still seems limited. I hope my education and intelligence will place me in

my dream position of employment…whatever that is.
- My worth – I am worth more than waiting for marriage. There is life to be lived and I will no longer chase after a man. I choose to chase after God because He knows my worth.
- My skills/abilities – I am all tapped out of school. (NO MORE) I think I have a range of experiences.
- My walk with God – Because of God and my choice to chase after Him, I feel the most WHOLE I have ever felt. I love God and my walk can always improve in my level of faith.

God's responses to the concerns that lay heavy on my heart were very direct. His voice and instruction was clear.

1. Think of yourself as I think of YOU!
2. Encourage yourself (Life of David)
3. Build yourself-esteem (Life of Jeremiah)
4. Affirm yourself when you've missed it (Life of Peter)
5. Accept yourself in the midst of rejection (Life of Leah)
6. Spend time in MY presence for wisdom about your life (Life of Hannah)
7. Take time out just for you when others are pulling on you (The Life of Jesus)

And so, I began to read about each individual's life to gain a greater perspective of what God was saying to me. By the end of the evening, I left my thoughts, desires, and worries in my journal with the expectancy that God would navigate me. I felt peaceful and most of all relaxed! I looked forward to what my thirties had to offer. I made my way to church on Sunday to close the weekend appropriately. I remember thinking *I don't want to move from this space in the Lord. The hands of the world will be knocking at my door and I have the ability to choose whether or not I will answer with a smile and a servant heart or if I will just let em' knock because the moment is too good to be interrupted.* During service, I felt encouraged to give more in my offering than what I normally give outside of my monthly tithes. I increased my offering so that my faith would be increased. At that moment, I said to God, "I am trusting that the doors of promotion, opportunity, and increase have opened for me because your word, in which I have meditated on says,

You will increase me more and more, me and my children
(Psalms 115:14)

"I believe, I see it, and I am experiencing the manifestation!" was my confession. Eight months later I was confronted with an opportunity in my faith/walk with the Lord to definitely increase and promote me to a new spiritual level.

***

My Dad came to live with me for four months. I got the opportunity to meet the inner man for the first time. Daddy had been a substance abuser all my life and now his soul was begging for freedom. Guess who would be forced to step up to the plate. You got it, me! It was no wonder I was battling with a dismissive attachment behavior toward men. To say the least, during my childhood Daddy and I had our moments of coloring, drawing, playing cards, and stealing hubcaps. I remember my Dad helping me with my math homework and always giving me affirming speeches, like, "Tori, you know this. You're smart 'lil girl'. (chuckle) You take just after your Daddy." Then I would respond, "Well, what I get from my Momma?" The man's humor is never-ending; everything is a joke to him. He would say, "You know when you can't get your way and you make that face when you're unhappy and you start to pout? That! You little brat!" Those conversations would always continue with a back and forth debate about why I get everything "good" from him and everything "bad" from her. We *still* have those conversations.

During those intimate times he would leave in the middle of a card game, or one of our intense matches of chess. Other times he would leave in the middle of a TV show we were watching together, or in the middle of a conversation. I would become angry with him when he would nod off on me. As a little girl, I would yell, "All you ever think about is what's in them streets and chasing money!

That is more important to you then spending time with me. My Momma was right!" Oh boy, those words would definitely get my Dad's attention. He would respond with just enough emotion to silence me and give himself time to escape out the backdoor. If the moment was full of too much guilt, I got to tag along. Most of our trips consisted of going to different houses within a two to three block radius. Some blocks away, other neighborhoods away or houses away.

On a few of our trips, I was the watch girl and thrilled about it. Watching my Daddy pop off other people's hub caps on their cars and escape in pure fear of getting caught is memorable for me. *But why would he have to steal hub caps when he has a job?* I thought. Daddy has worked for Ford Motor Company since I can remember. I suppose Ford wasn't paying him enough. Silly little girl.

"I am not prepared for this Lord! I can't take care of his medical needs while he is detoxing! Ok, what do you want me to do Lord? Whatever it is, you're going to have to give me strength." And for the next four months of my life, I dated my Dad. Every little girls dream is to be complimented by her Daddy; affirmed by her Father; identified by his name, which should naturally transition from Dad to Husband. Within those four months, my Dad and I went back and forth about our philosophies on life, prayed together, chatted about men, went to the movies, went to dinner, cooked dinner, traveled, talked much about the past and fights he and my mother had, shared some laughs and eventually cried together.

Where have you been all my life, man? Even when you were right there, you were not there and now, you are right here and there is nowhere for you to go or for me to go. I was overwhelmed! For women who have never met their father, cannot imagine a relationship with their Dad for whatever reason, or have lost their father; you have not lost "our" Father, the Lord Jesus Christ.

During my Dad's addiction, I could have easily testified to not having a Dad or identified with the idea that he was an absent father because his focus was not on fathering most of the time. Even still, I turned to God many of nights with tears, frustration, prayers over his life, for affirmation for my identity, comfort for my worries, nurture for my needs and He was always there for me. I can honestly say it is no cliché that the Lord will *never* leave you or forsake you (Deuteronomy 31:6-8, Joshua 1:5, 1Kings 8:57, 1Chronicles 28:20, Psalms 37:28; 94:14, Isaiah 41:17; 42:16, Hebrews 13:5); that He will be your mother and your father when you believe that your mother and your father have forsaken you (Psalm 27:10). The key for me was to believe that those words we sing and hear in songs like *Hallelujah Anyhow*, were true. At this point in my life I had experienced many hits to my identity. I was accused of being sexually active by my Mother.

I was identified by my mustache in high school. I learned when people talked about me, they used the description, "The light skinned girl with the mustache?" Even though getting rid of my mustache was the best thing I could have done for my outer identity, it was the hardest thing I have ever had to accept, but the process was necessary for my change. And I was told by Charlie that my personality was up and down. With my Dad as my new roommate, I believed I had nothing else to lose. Who knew my thoughts would soon prove not to be true?

Could it be because I was in a place of control and in a role of authority that I did not want to be in? What I needed from him as a child and what he needed in that moment from me were two different things. I did not think I was angry with him, although my actions did display discontentment at times. I was aggravated by his neediness. Man, this was me! I was needy too! I was looking in a mirror and finally realized I needed to show love and positive regard. *I AM A COUNSELOR!* I'm not supposed to counsel my family. My Dad was shifting back and forth from wanting to live to wanting to die because of the pain he was experiencing in his stomach and the knowledge of knowing others who were experiencing detoxification from heroine were dropping dead like flies around him. I had a responsibility and that was to speak life into my Daddy's life and show God's love to a man who was probably doing himself more detriment mentally than I could ever do verbally or emotionally.

It was not time for me to get revenge and make him suffer for the suffering his absence caused me. This frustration was not good for either one of us and I for sure could not counsel myself.

I recognized that in this time God planned for us to have what we both needed – to heal.

I stopped focusing on his sickness and allowed God to shift my eyes towards his soul and his heart. My needs were supplied. I was grateful, that in that very moment of caring for my Dad, the need to be validated by a man was lost. My father said to me that I was pretty and smart, I deserved the best, and I would make any man happy. He told me that I was going to be a great wife and mother, he was blessed to have a daughter like me who cared for people, that I was great at my job, and I was strong.

Although my Dad was affirming me, God had already filled my cup with validation. I was just now recognizing the work completed in me through my Dad's affirmations. The validation from my Daddy was like cocoa butter on a healing scar. I lost the need to be validated by my Dad as I gained validation from my Dad through my Father. Thank you Lord.

Powerful Love

In the presence of powerful love, humility is of no existence shared by two who believe in persistence;
Nor does it exist when one has realized the pain that caused the ache in the stomach, the emptiness in the heart, the illusions in the mind and the soul wondering why?
Why does times get so rough?

> *Why does the war seem so tough to fight that victory over the battle seems like an illusion of hope that was created by this dope?*
>
> *That love dope is a powerful drug & humility is of no existence in the presence of powerful love.*

Even though I was appreciative of the time Daddy and I shared, taking care of him during his process was heavy for me. In addition to the disorganization I experienced in the school halls, I was more than overwhelmed. Spring break could not come fast enough. I needed another one of my excursions to get a break. Had I plotted to detour from my time changing life focus? What was I headed for during Spring break and who was I headed to this time? I relapsed into looking for male validation and avoidance behavior. Next assignment…

Las Vegas

I would quit my job in April of 2011 as a school counselor to begin my new career. I was about to receive the job I had sowed into and confessed during my birthday weekend at church. My Dad and Cayenne had become nerve wracking. Mommy was leaving Cayenne with dear old Granddad for a few days, to escape to Las Vegas.

I met up with a couple of college friends, Lyla and Jaime. In between life happenings (marriage, having babies, jobs, family drama, and relocations) the girls and I tried to remain connected with spontaneous trips. Sometimes it would be three of us, other times it was two of us going on excursions together. Very seldom, was the five of us able to get together (Me, Lyla, Jaime, Mena, and Sheryl). For the most part, those times are only around Christmas and New Year's.

***

At first we called ourselves the "Fab Five". Now our Google group email identifies us as "Real Friends 5". We are all different in many facets, but the one constant among us is our faith in God. In college, our philosophies on life were not too different from one another. Of course, our backgrounds, experiences, and education had given us multiple perspectives to view life through; but the basis of our beliefs, regardless of how our beliefs manifested themselves in our ritualistic behaviors, was that God is real and is intricately involved in all of our separate but common lifestyles. For that reason and others, I believe is why my friendship with the girls has sustained itself for over 15 years.

Mena is from Detroit and attended the almighty Cass Technical High School. You can go anywhere in the country and say you are from Detroit and the next question people will ask is what high school did you go to because they knew someone who went to Cass.

Cass was the top school in the public school system and Mena was every bit of a result of their high standards. She was raised by her grandparents in a household with strong Christian values. She is a walking encyclopedia. Although, I hated when she corrected my vocabulary! It was bad enough I was struggling in that area. I did not need her to correct me.

I had a French class with Jaime during my freshman year and her sophomore year. Jaime was not too friendly but I did not care, I spoke to everyone who looked like me at my predominantly white school. She was from Cleveland Heights, a very supportive family background, and spoiled. I could never figure out why we argued so much but then it hit me... we were both spoiled and catered to by our parents! Who knew that that was our reality that possibly connected us and disconnected us at the same time?

Lyla was from Cleveland too. Mena was specific about distinguishing Cleveland from Cleveland Heights. She did not care too much for Jaime saying she was just from Cleveland because there was a big difference of living experiences within a city. For instance, Detroiters scorn people who say they are from Detroit when they are really from the suburbs of Detroit. Yes, we understand the nature of proximity and how it can be a hassle to explain an unfamiliar area to people who do not get it; so to avoid all the turns of trying to explain your actual residence, it is easier to say the larger city, which provokes the disdain. Those who live within the inner city have a unique living experience from those who live outside the inner city.

Mena was very intentional about making Jaime mindful of that, I am just not sure if Jaime cared. Lyla on the other hand never seemed to jump in to add her spin on the outlook. When Lyla did speak, we all looked at each other in bewilderment as if to say, *"What is she talking about?"* Lyla was from a two-parent household with strong Christian values as well. She was the oldest of four with three younger brothers. We believed Lyla was sometimes slow to catch on to the point of a story, but not too much of anything would go over her head. She was quite the observant one.

And there was Sheryl: a tall framed, strong voice, track-runner. When I met Sheryl, I was actually uncomfortable. I was being exposed for the first time to a black girl who "talked white." I was in awe that she was as articulate as she was and friends with the others. Sheryl was from a city about forty five minutes from Cleveland and a two-parent Christian household too. I do not know if I felt more uncomfortable about being the minority amongst the new girls I started to call friends in a place far from home, or because everyone came from a household I only fantasized about. Even Mena having relationship with her maternal grandparents was something I silently envied. The value of the circle became the identity of the circle and ultimately is what kept us connected:

1. Our faith in God and
2. Our self-actualization.

Each of us was clear on who we were regardless to what type of home life we came from. It was evident to me that within this circle of friends none of us tried to be another or be better than the other. We all were trying to be the best "us" we could be with all of our flaws. I was able to have a deep respect for each of the girls which caused for me to believe that I could trust them. Most women experience difficulties in relationships with one another because of our narcissistic ego. Jealousy and competition, both stem from a place of low self-esteem and a lack of self-love. As a group, that was not us. We did not attack one another to outdo the other. Now let's not misunderstand what I am saying. At some point, I believe all women experience a lowered self-esteem and compromise self-love. If you want to know where a woman's focus is as it pertains to herself, watch her patterns. If the patterns are negative, more than likely, the behaviors derive from an internal place due to an external locus of control and are being externally demonstrated as an indirect impact, which hurts you. The behavior I am referring to that is "not us" is the behavior women are stereotypically known for displaying in friendship groups that causes women to not value relationships with other women such as directly hurting someone else because of your own self-disgust. It has been my experience that amongst these four women I call friends, I have always been able to be myself and that is a value for me.

***

We had a ball in Las Vegas. I had worked with kids carrying inherited baggage for four months and I wanted to party! Michael Jordan stayed in our hotel. His celebrity golf tournament was taking place throughout our stay in Vegas and *we* were "in the house". Our first night in town I met James. From the moment I stepped foot in Vegas I was on the move and ready to dance. The Ariel Hotel has a club on its top floor where the beats resound to the bottom floor. After the ladies and I graced our room with our luggage, we headed straight to an open eatery. The girls were hungry but I was too excited to eat. After sitting at the table bouncing to the jams that were being played above my head, like ole school Rob Base, I ran back to the room for a quick bath and to change my clothes. I was walking in the door as the party was ending. "Is the party over?" James, who was exiting, asked, "You wanna go somewhere else? I know a place where we can go." His buddy said, "Yeah, there's a party in room…" and gave what I believe to be his room number. I punched him in his chest and said, "Excuse me? What do I look like to you?" This was of course, after James looked at him and said, "Man…", with a look of disappointment. After I got the impression that even James thought his buddy's comment was uncouth I sized this short, pudgy, well-groomed man up and down and thought *He seems safe*. "I'll go with you but you gotta drop your buddy." I wasn't feeling his vibe. James was nicely dressed in a suit and tie, which nowadays does not mean usually anything but a brotha can dress. His black shoes caught my attention though. Not too dusty and not too shiny, square toed that said, "I work a lot in these shoes." I figured he was in Vegas for the same reasons I was in Vegas – to escape from work.

"Where are we going?"

"I know this lil place in the Bellagio" and off we were transported by a limo. I remember thinking to myself, *Okay, who is he? Or does everyone roll around in a limo in Vegas?* James was a perfect gentleman and to my surprise a recent youth pastor at a Catholic Church. "I recently submitted my resignation as youth pastor because I was the only black man working in a church that did not seem to give me opportunities for advancement." He was frustrated with being stifled and had had enough of church politics. I wondered if he was in Vegas to spiritually rebel. I was there to rebel against patience.

Of course I asked him. "I haven't looked at it that way before. I don't know."

We were up until 6 o'clock the next morning talking, laughing, and sharing our stories, which led to a little counseling – it is hard to leave home without it. Counseling is like a silk blouse that sticks to my skin in the summer when it is hot. No, he was not in Vegas to spiritually rebel. He was accompanying a friend on a business venture. When he discovered that I was a counselor working on my Ph.D., he seemed to be even more interested in my wit, intellect, and ability to challenge him in a conversation.

He was intrigued, which left me to wonder, *Women like me don't come to Vegas often, huh?* He went on to tell me all about the comedy show Kevin Hart hosted for Michael Jordan. He showed me the pictures he took with celebrities and with his buddies. "Hey! Do you wanna go to Michael Jordan's golfing event with me tomorrow?"

"Yes! But I'm here with my girls and I can't leave them like that. I already left them tonight. But I wanna go! I can only go if my girls can come too. We came together and to me, that wouldn't be fair." James hemmed and hawed for minutes about how he wasn't sure if he could get two more passes. "You can work it out!" I said confidently. Three hours of sleep later and James was calling my phone asking, "How soon can ya'll be ready?" When I came in the room that morning the girls were worried about where I had been all night. I erased their concern when I told them we were going to Michael Jordan's Celebrity Golf Tournament. Chauffeured in a limo, we all thought the trip could not get any better. We stayed at the golf tournament all day. Jaime took pictures of all the celebrities with her high class camera.

From the pictures she took, you would have thought we were right there in their personal space. While watching from afar, in the shaded stands, James demanded my attention and asked, "Can I take *you* to dinner tonight?"

The girls overhearing James' request responded, "Yes!" Once we returned from the event, I was to freshen up and change clothes to meet James in the lobby because we were going to see the Lion King on Broadway. We had discussed during our late night conversation what the girls and I were doing in town. I explained we were there to see a few shows, enjoy good food, and win some money.

I told James about wanting to see The Lion King and how Lyla said the show was "a must see." He expressed the same excitement and desire to see the show. I did not use to be like this, I was a good girl, close to wholesome, and I never shaved my hairy legs but I put on one of my dresses to show them off this evening. On my way to meet James I met my date for the next day; a clean, well groomed, nice smelling, sharp "ole G." He was a fish I should have thrown back. He stared at my legs, then my eyes and asked as if he knew me, "Where are you going?"

"I'm on my way to a show." We dialogued briefly about who we were with, why we were in Vegas, and our plans. Lyla caught up to me and brought my eyeglasses because I would not have been able to see in the distance. I must have left them in my haste to be on time meeting James to make a good impression. Tiger asked, "You're going to a show with a guy?" *I'm free and had started to become happily single.*

"Yes I am, but we can go out tomorrow." I could not give the Lion King a fair share of my attention; how rude was I to fall asleep on this man and his $100 tickets! It was his fault that I was tired from hanging out all night and all morning, my body was calling for rest. This night of adventure could not end soon enough, as my eyes were calling for the heavenly bed in my room. After leaving James, I met the girls at another hotel for a show of our own, the *Thunder from Down Under*. At the end of our show, we agreed to meet James and a few of his friends at Caesar's Palace to tour the town and take pictures. Jaime is a photographer and this part of the evening added to her thrill in Vegas. (Speaking of pictures, I still have not gotten copies of those memorable photos.)

Four hours into my rest and our room phone rang. Lyla answered and I heard her say, "Oh, you want Tori."

My voice was froggy. I was just falling into a deep sleep.

"You're still asleep?"

"What else am I suppose to be doing?"

"Oh wow, I'm sorry… I was hoping you would join me for breakfast."

"Who is this?"

"Tiger."

"Oh… I'm sorry. Sure, I'll meet you downstairs in 20 minutes."

I jumped out of bed, gargled, and freshened up with a squirt here and there. I threw on some jeans and one of my newly bought Michael Jordan Celebrity golf polo shirts. Jaime was not happy with me. I did tell her before we even stepped foot in the city that I was coming to shake the city, meet some guys, and have a good time. My exact words were, "Don't be surprised, but you may see a different me." My adventurous excursions led to some heavy intense conversations with the girls later… but, we got over it. We always do.

During breakfast, Tiger was open about his past, which actually scared me and I do not scare easily. I was raised by Sabrina's Momma remember and had taken Daddy's 101 schooling on how to hustle and never go broke. His past lifestyle sounded dangerous and I was not sure he had totally escaped from his past. I was too afraid that his past life would at some point meet up with him in his present and I did not want to be anywhere in sight! I suppose Tiger assumed his story would intrigue me. We shared a meal once more during my stay and talked for a month and half afterwards. Maybe I was intrigued. At 47, Tiger was the oldest man I had ever considered hanging out with. It was not going to work; he was smooth and the daddy that I did not need. My own Daddy was at home waiting with Cayenne. When I got back he was more vibrant than I had ever seen him. We talked about my trip. I shared with him about my experiences with James and Tiger. Of course, he was surprised that I liked older men but totally got it.

More so, he was in awe of how I managed to bring home close to the amount of money I left with. Outside of our conversations about me, we *transitioned* to the topic of "the move."

A little less than a year later I relocated for a promotion. My Dad was living in a men's shelter that would adequately serve his needs and fill his spirit man. I had peace but yet, was still not fulfilled. Much self-reflection was taking place and Charlie and I were dancing to Adele's tune *He Won't Go*. I started to wonder "What am I not getting? What am I missing Lord?" I was at the point in my life where I had accumulated one semester of teaching as an Assistant Professor of counseling at a predominantly white university. I had purchased a new car, paid off some bills, calmed my escaping down and pretty much thought I had arrived. After classes my body longed for my dark space, under my covers. My body was tired from running in an emotional marathon but the duplex I lived in had no tub for me to SOAK! What was I thinking? Baths are my therapy!

6 ... STABILITY!

Jamaica

I intended for my visit to Jamaica to be a time for another "Come to Jesus" meeting. I needed to relax, to clear my head, tan, and talk to *Writing*. I was seeking direction again. I needed God to navigate my soul, my path, my thoughts, *a-gain*. I was in dire need for God's light to be a lighthouse within me as I pursued a new career and a new direction of life for my heavy heart. I had moved around so much that I was unable to be stable. I traveled with a young lady that I had just met in my new city through my hair stylist. I probably spoke to *Writing* one time.

According to my history of traveling, the first night always seems to determine the entire trip. Jan did not know me, so I prepped her on the plane. "Hey, I am so ok if at any time during the trip, you want to do your own thing, because there may be sometimes where I may get to myself and do nothing.

But I am willing to do whatever... you wanna do to celebrate your birthday – this is your weekend!" She was understanding and agreeable. "Alone time is good, while even on a trip with a traveling buddy." I was glad she understood.

    Our first night began with trying to get a taxi to Paradise Island, where it was ladies night. The frugal me was not happy that we missed the shuttle. I was determined to get us a free ride by the doorman but he was not going for it. We stood in the foyer of the hotel talking up a plan, when four beautiful men stepped out of a taxi van approached us with "Good evening Ladies. Where are you headed?" We headed into the hotel's lounge area with the four gentlemen to become acquainted. While standing in the lobby, we all shared our occupations and where we travelled from. Jan referred to them as The *Wolf Pack* from Barbados. Sanjay was a happily married commercial real estate agent with yellow skin that resembled yellow milk. The top of his head was smooth "like a baby's bottom" as he glided his fingers along his cranium. Sanjay, in my opinion was the one who kept the group in order. While I was once dancing with Peter (an unwedded man), in his prurient way, Sanjay stepped in to correct Peter's behavior saying, "A, no. You don't dance like that with a lady." At that moment, I remember thinking *God sends Angels wherever I go to protect me. What is wrong with my own voice?* Later I thanked Sanjay for stepping in as a big brother would and declared that he was the leader. He smiled and returned a thank you for the compliment or I suppose, role.

Peter I could tell was a money maker; he was into the insurance business. In his strong Indian accent he informed me that he was a father of three children between two women. I asked, "How come out of the four of you, you're the only one not married?" His response was vague but personal, I could tell. I imagined he wanted stability but was too busy enjoying life. He ascribed to being a great father and provider, "None of my children or 'baby's mama's want for nothing." He looked at me with lusting eyes, "I can teach you…" the start of his statement to my expression of excitement when I learned that they were going golfing the next day. The guys invited us to the course, Peter invited *me* to breakfast, both Jan and I gladly accepted. I had had enough of venturing out on my own from Vegas. I vowed to myself that wherever I went, Jan went also.

Since Vegas, I had become known for going on trips and not spending money, well, at least coming in under budget. That next morning, Jan and I met Peter for a breakfast of oatmeal and toast for me until Peter told me if I ate the toast with my oatmeal I would be doing my body an injustice. "If you want to give your body the nutrients it needs, eat the oatmeal alone." No debate. I trusted his statement, especially after seeing his arms. At 47, his arms were firm as steel. I quickly put the toast back. Apparently, meeting older men was becoming a pattern during my escapes. Something else I would need to reflect upon. After breakfast, Peter asked us to meet them in the lobby for a day of golfing.

While the guys golfed, Jan and I took advantage of the golf lessons Peter and Sanjay arranged for us. I felt like a pro behind the way my body ached afterwards. To thank the guys for a fun day, we drove a caddy around looking for the food stand to purchase lunch. Unbeknownst to us, the guys had already raided the food stand and were planning *our* evening together.

The evening after golf, the guys escorted us to a dinner off the dock, where the breeze from the water surrounded us. My salmon with mushrooms, rice and I'm sure some form of mixed vegetables, was delectable. My stomach would not allow me to finish my food. I hate wasting food! But I had already eaten too much. Immediately after dinner, on the dock, our table was removed and the area was transformed into a dance floor. The weather was moon lighting. The wind was calm and the night was still young. By the end of the night, Peter and Kwami were walking us to our room as our bodyguards. I wondered was the walk to ensure that 'we made it safely' or did they think they were in store for a night cap?

***

Kwami was a doctor of medicine, and apparently not in a good place in his marriage. He was gorgeous; tall, nicely built with beautiful smooth milky brown skin and pearly white teeth. During the day, while the other's explored sports, Kwami interviewed potential nurses for his practice.

He was dangerous and always flashing his married pearly whites in my face. One night as we were on our way to dinner with the fellows, after getting annoyed with his flirting, I screamed, "YOU-ARE-MARRIED and I do not play with God and the covenant of marriage!" He debated with me but soon shared a level of respect that I will always appreciate. Upon the end of their trip when we all departed and wished each other safe arrivals back home Kwami remarked, "Ok, Tori. You're tough and that's good. Don't ever change who you are."

***

Once we reached our room door, our last words were "Thank you and good night." My identity was not about to take another hit from my escapes. Although, something was quite heavy on me that night and I tossed and turned in my bed. In the wee hours of the night I escaped to the hotel steam room to soothe my raging hormones. The next day, Jan and I traveled into town to shop! She was adamant about getting coffee from Jamaica. I could not understand how serious it was to her; I am not a coffee drinker, I just drink coffee; therefore, I could not relate. When we returned from our day of adventure, we agreed that our bodies needed to soak in the hot tub from the long day of walking. Initially, we had a hard time finding the small tub amongst all the other water surrounding our resort. We noticed the lights coming from the ground and ran to lull our bodies into the warm waves of the jets.

We must have soaked for two hours reminiscing about how much fun the guys were, how respectful they appeared, and how they insisted on taking care of us. I gave an example.

Back at the hotel after golfing, I went to the bar to get some ginger ale for the irritating allergic reaction my throat was experiencing. While at the bar I bumped into Peter and Sanjay who were having a drink. "Tori! How are you doing? We enjoyed you ladies today!" Sanjay was enthusiastic. "Hey fellows! We had a good time too. I'm not doing too well. I think I'm getting sick. My throat feels scratchy."

"Noo. I wonder if it was the grass from the course. Bartender, can you get the lady a hot whiskey with honey and lemon? Thank you."

"After you drink that you should be fine" Peter piped in.

"I hope so."

The three of us talked for a good 30 minutes, long enough for me to feel nice after having two hot totty's. While soaking in the warm water, Jan and I asked each other "Are all men of Indian descent kind like this?" We were overwhelmed with their attentiveness, yet grateful for their accommodating nature. Kwami's mother was Indian and his father was African American. Peter was full Indian. Sanjay and Shev were Kenyan, though looking at Shev you would have assumed he was a White man from London with a British accent. Physically drained from the heat, we headed back to our room.

Walking across the lobby, we bumped into Peter and Sanjay for another invitation to dinner. This was the guys last night in town. I pulled Sanjay to the side and shared that Jan's birthday was the next day. Since this was our last night hanging out with them, I wanted to make the night special for Jan. I could tell, she had never been open to meeting and hanging out with strangers but she had admitted that this new experience was one of the greatest times of her life. In her email she sent to everyone with a link to view her online pictures from our trip, she shared, "Meeting and spending time with all of you is an experience I'll cherish. Thank you for making my birthday the most memorable to date. Thank you for touching my life."

The restaurant was on a boat that seemed like it rested in the middle of the ocean. We had to take a ferry to get there. The ambiance was dim lighting, candlelit tables, quiet and quaint. I remember Shev, who was maybe 52, making a toast, "You two are good girls and have made this trip so much better. We should do this again!" We laughed and I thought about how nice spending time with the guys actually was for me. In many ways they had affirmed my identity of being a good girl again. Concluding our toast, our waiter brought a piece of cake with a candle to the table to greet and wish Jan a happy birthday. She tear'd up. Her moment was made special. We took random photo shots, enjoyed our meal and a casual argument between Peter and Kwami. No one knew why the two of them were arguing or how the argument even began; but no one seemed to care either.

We were having a grand time, laughed hard, and talked more. From the boat house, we continued our celebration back at the hotel in the lounge with the cleaning crew. Every person danced and sang most of the night while Jan and I snapped random photos of memorable moments.

Home from Jamaica, and I grieved returning to work. I started viewing my job, career, and my desires differently. I could not stop thinking of how rejuvenating the trip actually was for me. I began researching guest lecturing opportunities out of the country and reaching out to contacts that had connections overseas for possible job opportunities. I was unsettled with life once again. As much as I longed for stability, I could not keep my fanny still. I was aching to escape my current place of employment while my search for fit became intentional and my body cried out for fixing. From all of the driving and flying, I was backed up with tensed muscles and a misaligned pelvic bone that needed released. The option for me to take nightly baths did not even exist, so I laid on a table three times a week for my inflaming sciatic nerve! I was trying to relax my tension and imagine a master plan for my life through the encouragement of smooth melodies in the dark massage room lit by fake tea lights. One day my massage therapist quietly shared she was dealing with a "separation" as I was trying to forget about my own relational departure.

I assumed she and her significant other were breaking up or just having a back and forth moment in the relationship, (you know, when it's not really over). I listened with the intention to ONLY listen because, *I was getting treatment* and I wanted to relax.

When she said they had been together for nine years as boyfriend and girlfriend, my heart and ears perked up and I went into recovery zone. Where are my life jackets? She was definitely broken. I thought I had just the life jacket she needed. Maybe I was in the "right place at the right time". After putting my needs to the side, I said, "I know what you're going through." She seemed shocked because she said, "Really?"

"Yeah", I said. "You've been in an unlawful marriage where you believed and waited and maybe planned to get married, which is why you stayed."

"Yeah, and kept the house clean, cooked, and moved out of my house that *I* bought before we were dating... That's the very reason why I'm leaving because we're not."

"And you feel empty… As women, we want to be guided. We need to be protected. We have to be able to trust."

"It's hard. With my shitty upbringing, now I have to move back in with my parents. Someone lives in my house. I don't know what to do. And I know that it's over because he's not the type to come after me. He has too much pride for that." She cried.

I was all too familiar with her story. What do we do when life does not go as we planned?

After the unfulfilled promises, after the beautiful wedding dress we walked down the aisle in and now the divorce is final, after bringing the baby home to discover that those same problems are still there looking you dead in the face "cross-eyed", what do you do? Think about the many marriages ending in divorce, the extreme numbers of single mothers raising children, the growing numbers of professional women being career driven while hungering for family yet, not going after it for fear of losing self-arrival? Independence? The "I have a Dream" speech for my life? Or not able to go after marriage and a family because you are loving the wrong person? Are your eyes fixated on the wrong things that only bring conditional happiness?

Think about the many women who are trying to do it all with the roles of being a wife, mother, community activist, while having a career and still trying to figure out herself. You may be the woman who believes you are doing it right, has it going on, got the man, got the degree, got the dream job, may or may not have the children and is okay either way and you are saying to me, "I don't know what you're talking about lady, I'm good. I can't relate." Sure you are, maybe in those areas but who do you say that you are; all of those things that you have collected, like a pirate? You have the man but is he your husband? Or have you been dating and playing house for umpteenth years too? If he is your husband, is he your first love, your only love, or one of your many loves? How is your soul doing? Is it hungry? Might it be starving? Mine was.

Women need direction and guidance from men! Men have a distinct role in the lives of women. Fathers give their daughters an identity, their first family name. With the right amount of healthy affection, time, and affirmation fathers provide their daughters with a well-balanced sense of self, offering a set of secured emotions. When fathers provide consistent expressions of love and fulfillment of their daughter's needs, I think it's safe to say, those daughters know the experience of stability and do not have to bounce around looking for it. At least, this is my story. Once the daughter develops into womanhood, after puberty, she dreams of being chosen by an acceptable fellow who will love her and provide for her as her father did or should have done. When a man identifies himself as the one who wants to commit to the woman (as her husband), his responsibility is to then take over the father's responsibility in providing for his daughter, *as her husband* – that is, providing the woman he marries with *his* identity (last name), security (taking care of her needs), and stability (consistently providing expressions of love and care), all of which I searched for and was unable to find.

I believe women become lost or lose touch with self and the purpose of our existence when we may not have received the appropriate, healthy messages from our Daddy. Because my young massage therapist spoke about an unfair upbringing she so vividly described, I imagined she did not get from Daddy what she was hoping to find in her man friend, who probably missed adequate affirming messages himself.

I thought about Charlie and how I could not be mad at him nor should he be mad at me for the way we were raised. She could not be mad either, so I challenged her to discover more of herself through envisioning dreams unfulfilled, places untraveled, and goals yet attained. "Don't get bitter, get better!" I told her. "Can I pray with you?"

When God tells you to be okay with your current position and it can accurately be described as a whirlwind…how can you have and maintain peace within? You may think you cannot; yes you can. I did not think I could neither. As a matter of fact, I did not want to have peace because like my massage therapist, I was mad at life not happening how I imagined. Now, I wanted to escape again. I had become a good little escape artist, running from anything that looked like pressure and stick-to-itiveness. I ran from Charlie. Charlie ran from me. I ran from my family and their emotional roller coasters. I ran from any man who thought he wanted to marry me because of the pressure of the idea of actually having what I always wanted, but from who, you? I ran from God as much as I thought I was running toward Him. And then He grabbed me and held me tight. I could not run anymore. There was no place to go. My intelligence had overanalyzed any possible option as nothing new.

Many people like to rest and think on the commode. One dreary day after having a luxurious protein breakfast with a scrambled cheese egg with garlic, salt and Cayenne, three pieces of Cayenne bacon, and a handful of grapes with some tasty crystal purified water, I was full. I was figuratively full and needed to let go of garbage within in me. I cried out as hard as I could.

How can I be okay with where I am when my father doesn't have a place to call his own? How can I be okay with where I am when my mother is texting me nasty messages about how I'm addicted to being perfect and I need to come down from my high horse?

How can I be okay with where I am when my nephew is searching for his identity, trying to identify with quick money schemes that only provide a false sense of identity and status that has been glamorized by media and fake mentors in the streets?

HOW CAN I BE OKAY WITH WHERE I AM when every time I go into a class to teach I'm afraid I will be asked a question I CAN NOT ANSWER!

Was this what I had waited for once the PhD was complete; students who would challenge my ability to check a paper, be rude while I spoke, question my authority and competence; colleagues who would professionally bully me; and an identity that I continued to question?

How can I be okay with where I am when I hate that I still love Charlie?

Was this what a life for me as a young black spiritual educated woman is all about?

And then Anthony Hamilton's song caught my attention from the living room *Fair in Love*. God used the lyrics in this song to speak to me. I heard God saying He was waiting on me to give up something in order to receive the love that was ready for me. "I hear you Lord." My thoughts screamed, *WHAT ELSE IS IT THAT I NEED TO DO?!* Then I went back to Writing to REFOCUS. Then Ledisi's song shuffled in on media player and told me to be good to myself. "Okay Lord!"

LOVE AND FREEDOM
7 LOST ON THE JOURNEY

I thought I *was* being good to myself. When I traveled, shopped, relaxed and even planned quiet time for myself. I organized my life and paid all my bills on time. I was financially at peace or at least financially disciplined. My tithes were paid consistently whether I was at church or not.
I took time to visit loved ones in my life.

For instance, after learning that Charlie's mother had experienced two strokes, I paid her a visit. I remember praying, "Lord, please don't take this man's mother away from him." I wondered how she was healing and if there was something I could do to help lift her spirits since our relationship had always been rocky.

I remembered the candy jar I had of Charlie's from his football years. This candy jar with plastered pictures of him playing football held many memories for me. What a perfect time to give the jar away and to his mother. I thought *if I give this candy jar to her as a gift, I'm more than sure this will lift her spirits.* I filled the jar with my favorite Dove chocolate candies. I love the inspirational messages on the wrappers. I wanted to pass on some inspiration, while at the same time leave a seed. During my check-in, we talked, laughed, she cried and talked about her son of course. One thing that struck me most of our conversation was her comment about why Charlie and I could not seem to get along. "I know my son loves you," she said. I have always believed that somewhere within Charlie's heart, there was a deep love for me. I was oddly at ease when Charlie's mom stated she believed "he loves you crazily." I was suddenly shocked when she said he and I could not get along because he cannot handle me always having something to say to demonstrate that I am smarter than him. Her statement was not a new revelation for me. Charlie had expressed similar words himself such as "You always have something to say." The new revelation was his mother's understanding of what she believed was wrong with our relationship. I was not sure what to think about what she shared considering throughout my relationship with Charlie, she had encouraged him to date other people.

 In that instance, I remember thinking, *why do I care what she thinks of me, who's affection am I trying to win anyway?* The process of detaching myself from personalizing people's opinions of me, I believe began to expand for me in that moment. I was awakened to how genuine and true my love for Charlie had always been, now through his mother's eyes. I was suddenly glued into how true and loyal I have always been to everyone in my life that I loved, especially my family. My eyes were able to see from my conversation with Charlie's mom, that there was nothing *terribly* wrong with me. I just loved hard. Maybe I loved too hard because *I* often walked away sorrowful from misunderstandings in my relationships. I *tried* to change myself to keep the relationships in my life but was *I really* okay? Just because I did what I perceived as "doing everything right" did not classify "me" as being okay with *me*. This revelation would be ignited even more when other relationships in my life became challenged.

***

On the job front, perplexity lingered around like an odor you beg to rid your nose from, like the smell of a rat! I was up for my first year evaluation as a Prof. For the past few weeks before the big day; I poured into making my portfolio well-organized, creative, and focused on areas of my work fellow colleagues would soon evaluate to determine if I was to keep my job or not. My mentors and past professors encouraged that I invest most of my energies into building a portfolio that represents promising scholarship. Well, to my best ability, I showcased my promising scholarship with my co-authored book chapter, my first single authored publication, and the two manuscripts that were in revision. As a first year educator, I was impressed with my own efforts. But it was not enough. The deliberation involved 10 of my colleagues, who discussed me while I waited in the hall. They determined that my low teaching evaluations did not meet their standard but could be improved with adequate mentoring. Their decision was a factor on whether or not I should be reappointed in my position for the following year. I received one abstention and one decline for reappointment in the vote. I was confused, disappointed, and lost. I felt out of place in this new environment I cautioned myself on calling home. The feeling of having no support from two colleagues, as a new faculty member hit me hard and would mimic what I would soon feel from other areas in my life. However, support from the eight colleagues who voted in favor of my reappointment unfortunately, did not lessen the blow.

I was isolated. The upheaval of emotions caused me to pour more into my students and build relationships around me that celebrated my presence. However, I was once again at a point where I needed to have another one of my *"come to Jesus meetings"*. This time it was about what and where I needed to be in life because 'happy' was just not willing to live at my address for a long period of time. It wasn't just because there was one person who didn't agree with me being a part of the department. It was the toxic influence that this one person created amongst others and their interactions with me. It was the smog of the office that embraced gossip, back-biting, and disrespect. It was the inappropriate conversations held with other colleagues and students that would support my isolation. It was the student evaluations adding to the fright of other's perspectives of me. And now, I was blind to where my support came from within my place of employment. The uncertainty forced me to press into God's presence even more. I cried, *"Why am I being persecuted Lord? What have I done wrong when all I thought I was doing was "the right thing"?* The holiday break could not come fast enough.

***

I was too excited about going home for the holiday and resting around family who celebrate me and look forward to my arrival. At least that was my hope. I arrived home a day before Thanksgiving, to assist Momma with her home make-over projects, as she was preparing her home for the first time to host family and friends for the holiday. We were all excited about the changes that were taking place in Momma's life. After the lawsuit from the car accident that fractured many places in her body, she purchased a house that she could finally call her own and then furnished the house with the additional payoffs. The day before Thanksgiving, my nieces and I were cleaning, cooking, and designing for the big day until 6am Thanksgiving morning. It started off as a memory to capture. Little did I know, I was in for a much bigger disastrous memory. Everyone woke up a few hours later to get back to work. I needed to stay in the bed for another hour or so because *I - was - exhausted!* I had a taxing experience at work, taught class until 10 pm the day I got on the road to drive home for the holiday, and immediately started working to assist with getting the house in order as soon as I stepped foot through the door. I had every right to be tired. As I lay in bed Thanksgiving morning, I could overhear Momma making sly comments about the work around the house no one was doing. So I called Breeze and AJ upstairs to ask each of them to complete a specific task that would add to making sure the house was ready for the arrival of company. I knew Momma had a foul disposition when I heard her remark, "See, don't *nobody* have to tell AJ to do anything. She sees something that needs done and she just do it." If I can remind you, AJ is my youngest niece, who is by the way, twelve and Breeze is eighteen. So we're talking about teenagers! - Who have to be told what to do because no kid in their right mind wants to work... especially on the holiday. I got up to finish what I started the night before but, I needed to eat first. Momma was in the kitchen preparing a plate of greens and cornbread to mash together and sprinkle a little hot sauce on, when I said, "I need to eat before I start working."

    She responded rather affirmatively with a nice gesture, "Go ahead and fix you something to eat." *Ok, she seems pretty cool based on her response,* I thought. So I started up a conversation with her about the cakes she was baking. In the middle of my asking about what type of cake she was planning to prepare, her plate of mashed up greens and cornbread slaps the floor. She goes off. Cursing, fussing, mentioning how everybody's just standing around on their phones doing nothing was all of the rants that proceeded from her mouth, as if, no one has done nothing at all. She became so irate that she screamed at me, "Get out of my face! Do something! Quit talking to me!"

What?!?! I'm sorry but what just happened? were my thoughts and from the looks of it, everyone else's who stood around the table. The girls were now looking at me incredulously as if to ask, "What did we do Auntie?" And she's STILL cussing and fussing walking around slamming cabinet doors and storming around creating a tense environment. I immediately thought *do not entertain her blow up, keep mopping the floor Tori*. But after listening to the words she chose to say, I started to feel my stomach curl and my blood boil. I was becoming upset because we were all there to help *her* prepare for *her* successful event and *her* attitude was pushing everyone away, once again. Her words she spoke underneath her breath indirectly to me, "…and you just now getting up" made me feel obligated to defend myself.

"I can't get some rest after just going to bed? I'm tired. I just drove two hours right after work to get here, what is the problem?" She threatened to knock me down. Supposedly, me, a thirty two year old woman, was back talking. Because I am an adult who respects her parents, I simply said, "It's time for me to go." Anytime another grown woman thinks that she is going to put her hands on me to solve a conflict, there will be no fighting. You see, Momma and Sabrina had exchanged threats, name-calling, and fists fights many times before. Not me. I would rather call the police and press charges – enough said. So since Momma is who she is, still emotionally disturbed, she had something to say about me saying it was time for me to go too.

"I don't give a [Fudge]! Leave! I don't need you doing a [Danish] thing for me!" Of course her words had no relation to food. And this was how my Thanksgiving Day started. Yet, I said, "Thank you Lord."

Once I returned to my quiet and peaceful home, two hours away from Momma, I made the decision to do some spring cleaning from emotionally draining relationships in my life. I was tired of feeling lost where I should feel loved. I blocked Momma from being able to call or text me because she was sending annoying, disrespectful, anxiety provoking absurd text messages. Whenever my phone alerted me that I had a new text message, my stomach curled into knots for fear of what I might read. I could not take it anymore. I had a conversation with Charlie that led me to believe I was going nowhere in my communications with him and it was finally time to get off and jump on a train that was headed in a direction I was trying to go. I created boundaries in my life that spoke the words loud and clear, I AM BEING GOOD TO ME FIRST! I was totally frustrated with *my* "Mother" and her emotional abuse that I said enough riding this roller coaster and anyone else's emotional roller coaster that had NOTHING POSITIVE to offer to my life and was only going down!

I cried to God even more, "What <u>have I</u> done wrong?" I thought I was doing everything right. My life feels unorganized; my bills are still paid on time; my tithes are always paid first. I save time, sow time, and spend time, which is Christian Life Center's motto. I serve others when time permits. I volunteer my time. I try to relax and take quiet time for me but my thoughts continue to flood my quiet space. I mean, I was using self-care "techniques", right? Why does my "self" not feel cared for? What am I missing? Then God whispered, "Me – You 'talk to me' but I wish you would talk more. I don't like to see you worrying. Let me show you how you don't have to worry. Trust me more, I am here." Embarrassed.

From that point on, I invested in my quiet time with God more than I had ever done in my life. Through meditations and silent readings, peace found me and **made** me still. I lost the need to have 'people' in my life for the sake of thinking I was not alone. I paid very close attention to God's presence in my life from the rising of the sun shining bright into my bedroom to the moon light permeating through my bedroom window as I laid in bed many nights thinking *what's next for me?* It was in those small moments of appreciation that I lost the need to save fragments of relationships while I marveled at God's relationship with earth and man. I had begun to acknowledge that I needed to trust God before I could even think about trying to trust people whose promises would always waver.

I lost the concept that family was only blood. God had placed so many beautiful people, *safe houses*, in my life whose love felt natural. I now understood how Jesus could tell the disciples, who pointed out that his mother and brother were amongst the crowd, *"My mother and brother are those who hear God's word and put it into practice"* Luke 8:21, New International Version (NIV). I began to see my life as not only a privilege to live but a privilege to be a part of. In order to live healthy we must eat healthy, associate with healthy people, meditate on positive things, exercise the body, maintain optimism in the midst of adversity and guard our thoughts and words. For *those who guard their mouths and tongues keep themselves from calamity* (Proverbs 21:23, NIV). Could this have been what Sabrina was trying to warn me of when she debated that my right hand should not tell my left hand everything? If people in my life who I loved so dearly were unable to contribute life, positive energy, or even reciprocate what I believed I contributed to their life, well, until God taught me how to better respond to hurting individuals who only demonstrated the language of hurt, all of their privileges were cut off until further notice. I had to keep myself from calamity.

During this time of **true** isolation, I studied the gospels in the bible. I studied the life of Jesus and his messages. I threw myself into my classrooms and pulled myself from bed. It was too easy to claim depression. Instead, I claimed freedom. I do not believe I have ever heard a statement that after fighting you would not feel exhausted. You *will be* exhausted. I was fatigued from cutting people out of my personal brain and heart space, which was more exhausting than I would have ever thought. I was releasing people, which means freeing them, right? These people were important to me, which made the fight more exhausting. I wanted to keep them, all of them. Although I desired to cry on Momma's shoulder for motherly nurturing when I felt alone, I could not. I wanted to hear a specific word of encouragement from Sabrina when I over-analyzed a situation, she was mute. I yearned for the warmth of Charlie's arms to embrace me with a hug when I felt pain, he was cold. I could not depend on none of them. I felt lost. I wondered, *"why me?"* In fact, asking the "why me" question was sequential based on all that had happened. After the breakdown of my personal and professional relationships I started asking myself too many "why" questions. "Why is this happening to me?" "Why do I have to endure this pain?" "Why do I feel alone but I am told that I am not alone?" Too many questions caused me to become overly-critical, overly-sensitive, and indulge in over-spending to satisfy my voids.

But God! Right before I headed down the wrong lane of self-pity and denial, God and the infinite charm God embodies reminded me of whose image I was created in *because* I cried out for God as I sat feeling alone. God comforted me like no other. Within days of my post-traumatic stress experiences, God intervened. A previous student sent an email expressing her appreciation of one of my classes. She exclaimed she learned so much and enjoyed my teaching style that she felt moved to offer me an invitation to stay at her parent's summer home in Key West. I was floored. But God! Another student gave me a gift of strawberry seeds with a note stating, "Keep planting seeds, even if you don't get the chance to see the seeds grow." I was more vigilant about my actions. But God! At the end of the year I sowed time with people in my life that celebrated my arrival, and took two of my nieces, my nephew, and my father on a road trip to Orlando, Florida for Christmas. I was intentional about where I invested my time and who I invested my time with. But God! Despite the detestable emails I received from a co-worker, I built relationships with my students and new colleagues in my workspace and developed a healthy working connection. I was now open to friendship from others surrounding my life. But God!

I will admit that I love roller coasters and sporting events which cause for me to strategize a reaction or an escape, such as paint ball. I love excitement! When I think about my search, I can identify the relationships that took me for long rides with deep dips and sharp curves I experienced in order to rise back to the top. I also can identify when I have been hit! In comparison to paint ball, being hit by paint really stings and can leave ugly bruises for days; in my case, months. Some of the hits I have taken from my own life journey have left some pretty blue bruises on my heart. As I reflect back, I often looked for what or who I thought would *add* to my life. People who would provide me with an identity; things that would provide me with stability; trust in those people *and* things I expected to provide me with security. My new found revelation became not to look for life in *people* and *things*, but to look for the one who gives Life and stay there.

Throughout your reading, what are some traits about yourself you were able to identify you lost while on your journey?

_____
_____
_____
_____
_____

What are some traits about yourself that you still need to lose?

_____
_____
_____
_____
_____

8 FOUND ON THE PATH

In everything that we do, we must remember that it is the responsibility of people to learn better ways of achieving and then pass the lessons on. Once we attain knowledge, we cannot keep it to ourselves. We must share how the understanding was gained in order to assist others facing similar tribulations.

While on my search for love and freedom, I recognized that the search started from taking notice of my unhealthy behaviors and beliefs that was learned through my parental training. I could not stop there. It was incumbent upon me to invest time in understanding how my parents paraded their own understandings of life that was healthy or unhealthy, yet assisting them in their own self-designed survival.

I had to ask hard questions, reflect, and be still. How do you explore fundamental areas of yourself without losing your mind? How do you self-evaluate critical areas of your life without giving your mind away? How do you develop balance in re-constructing your mind from parts of your up-rearing that may be hindering your self-growth? How do you re-construct your old belief system into a new system that results in healthy behaviors without going from one extreme to another?

If you have tried to escape your past and became a prisoner of it; if you have kept yourself busy to keep from working on you because of fearing the future; if you have sacrificed valuable time with time bandits; if you have become exhausted from all of the running around you do in your head, and are now ready to break free from the emotionally draining cycle, remain open and keep reading. To prepare for your next level of thinking and being, you cannot change everything at once. You cannot change behaviors and thought processes alone. Change should be done in small doses. You will need to identify safe houses to assist you. When identifying your internal struggles, you will need to tell yourself the truth as you self-evaluate your progress and areas for improvement.

To 'groom what you want to see bloom' you will need to change:

* in Small doses
* with Safe houses
* and Self-evaluate

If you are ready to do the work of re-constructing your mind and your heart – BRACE YOURSELF! It takes consistency with the small doses first. Small doses, in some cases, may be you just sitting with the knowledge of what is in need of change before doing anything. Do not wallow in sitting; yet, take notes about it. We have to become emotionally ready through becoming aware of our behaviors. We view the world from our experiences that will provide insight on the first steps we may need to take in changing our worldview. For example, if you believe that no one can be trusted because you have always experienced betrayal in your relationships, your worldview of people is warped. This sets you up to be deceived within your relationships because you have unhealthy expectations. I get it. You may argue, "Well that's all I've ever experienced is people lying and taking from me." In your mind, this justifies why you believe you cannot trust anyone. I hate to be the bearer of bad news but as my colleague Tish would say, "Ain't nobody thinking about you!"

People are consumed with their own lives. There is no one sitting around waiting to plot to deceive YOU of all people; unless your environment is full of deception. Those who are deceivers are plotting to deceive anybody, not just you. Check your inventory of relationships. Then look in the mirror.

Becoming aware of who you are, may consist of noticing the people in your circle, how hurtful your own words are, or how your behavior has caused pain for another person. The art of self-realization can be more powerful than feedback from others depending on how truthful you can be with yourself. Do not shy away from the truth. It is scriptural that the truth will **make** you free, *John 8:32*. What becomes most important is what you do with the new knowledge. If you allow the voice of God, which for some sounds like the voice of reason and wisdom, to lead you with specific instructions, you can begin the work of re-constructing your worldview. You have to commit to releasing your own will no matter how crazy you think you may look to others. God will never mislead you. Can you surrender your desires and trust that God will guide you to your desires? You want to be more than just 'happy' for a few moments? I do. You want joy to live in your heart? I do. No matter what society says you need to do, no matter what the economy is saying about your income, no matter what your family believes about your lifestyle, YOU want to be FREE. I do.

Next step... locate your safe houses. A 'safe house' can be a person or persons who ideally demonstrate a non-judgmental attitude toward you but support your process of growth. As you begin to look at yourself and uproot weeds, you will need help. I am reminded of the journey Africans endured while trying to escape racial terrorism in the southern states of America, before the Great Migration.

While on their journey, there were specific secretive symbols travelers were aware of, which indicated the people who lived in the homes were allies in support of their freedom from slavery. You too are a slave. A slave captured by an unproductive routine way of thinking that has produced unfavorable behaviors in your life. There are people waiting to help you toward freedom. Find them!

Pray with me that safe houses are provided for you or those in your life will become clear to you so you can begin your process with accountability that can be trusted.

> *Lord, I thank you for this moment of truth. I thank you for who you have created me to be even at this very moment, afraid of what's next but ready to trust you. Lord, send me help that I may become the person who I was purposed to be for this very moment. I love you and believe that you created me in your perfect image. Show me how to walk in love with my family. You gave them to me, show me how to love me the way that you love me, and let your will which is perfect be done in my life. Give me the eyes to see my situations how you see them, give me the ears to hear your voice so that I may be led by your voice only and the voice of a stranger I will not follow. I trust you Lord and am humbly surrendering to your will for my life.*
> *In Jesus name I pray.*
> *Amen.*

I am able to pray that prayer with you because one of my safe houses, Mom C., prayed that prayer with me often. The more we prayed, the more I became convinced that her motives were for my good. Now, write down the persons who came to mind after saying that prayer. Who did God show you while you were praying or after you prayed? What images did you see? Write your interpretation of why the persons or images were revealed to you. Is this person or are the individual's people of character that you admire and can follow? If so, pray and ask God for the words to say when having the conversation about where you are in life, where you are headed with God, and how you need their help. Just as Jesus traveled to spread the news about the kingdom of God, wherever He traveled there was always shelter provided, a safe place awaiting His arrival. Your safe place is waiting for you. Do not hold back – release everything and trust that God will never send you to a place where He will not keep you. No one is judging you but you. Begin to embrace the concept that God loves you and God knows you. Stop judging yourself so harshly. Though your previous behaviors have gotten you to a place of survival, now is the time for you to live.

As we become comfortable sharing our stories and being open to feedback, you mustn't stop self-evaluation nor should you become obsessed with it. There were times when Mom C.'s persistence made me think about how my behaviors and even my patterns caused people to see me in a way that I was not comfortable with.

I wanted to change but everything was happening so fast. I needed small doses of self-evaluation. I thought I had this reflection and transparency "thing" down pat when all along, I was on full and needed to release the garbage I held inside and protected for so long. Now that someone was prodding away at my garbage, I became protective of the nasty stuff and pulled away. I saw myself either becoming clingy to Mom C. or extremely void of emotion from my past. Thank God I was found. I needed balance within my thoughts and what God was doing in me and through me. I prayed and asked God about the feelings I was experiencing. I also realized that as much as I was grateful for my safe house and how Mom C. had instrumentally guided me through some dark places that my dependency needed to be upon God. It was hard because the emotional attachment to Mom C. was real and from a place of deep appreciation. I needed a healthy emotional attachment and you will too. I needed to not make my appreciation an unhealthy experience due to familiar relationship patterns. No one has ever loved me in a way that caused me to believe I owed them nothing in return besides my time. God's unconditional love found me at a fragile time in my life through one of His safe houses.

Because of my appreciation for the time Mom C. shared with me, I was fixed on proving to my safe house that I was changing from my old ways and was not trying to use them to take anything from her. But unbeknownst to me, I was needy for more time.

I took notice of how my thoughts wanted to manipulate the relationship for more time. I pulled back. I pulled back for the sake of not falling into old patterns. I pulled back to protect the relationship that had cultivated a woman of truth. I pulled back to prove to myself that I needed more time from God not man. I trusted God and found that God was waiting for me without judgment.

The goal of the journey is to become in tune with your Creator. Becoming attentive to God's voice empowers you to inevitably become attentive to yourself. This is the transformation you experience when you surrender your will for God's will. It is the ultimate experience when you choose to be molded and used by God. You have to be aware of your thoughts before they become your behaviors and before your behaviors become your character so that you can put on the character of God. Love.

In essence, your safe house is just what it is, a place of protective shelter that will provide you with tools for your continued journey. You will not stay there forever. You will need to gather yourself and all that you have become to move forward in your journey. There are lessons you will learn and the training you will receive will forever be imprinted on your heart because of the time invested; therefore, your safe house will always be with you. In many cases, she is the voice God uses to remind me of subtle standards I must uphold, such as "Don't accept crumbs from a man, you deserve the whole cookie sweet pea."

I must caution you on one thing: Trusting God in the safe house can be difficult because naturally, we tend to feed into our flesh more than our spiritual being. Trusting God must be the primary focus. Trust God, not the safe house alone. When I learned that there was someone I could be totally vulnerable with, my life truly took a turn for the better. She was the best friend I had searched for my entire life. I did not feel judged. My safe house encouraged me to be a better person. Soon, my thoughts tried to sabotage even this relationship; I knew God sent her to my life. I could not have noticed what was happening in me alone but with the Holy Spirit. I recognized I was becoming reliant on my safe house's prayers. At some point, I pulled back from doing the work that was necessary because the heat was turned up so high, I needed to breathe. Mom C. was persistent in eviscerating me. She was on her job and I knew it. For a minute, I felt like a plucked chicken with red bruises all over my body. My emotions had become sensitive to all that I had released because I held the belief *I was made like this and some of this works for me.* I was not too keen on my manipulative behavior, my neediness, and having to wait.

It is a process Tori!

As we prayed, who came to your mind? What character traits about this person or these persons are attractable to you? Are those traits Godly? Ask God what you should glean from the person(s) and take note...

9 CONFESSIONS OUTRO

I have no secrets is how I started this process and truth is what I will continue to seek throughout my development. As soon as I believe I have overcome one childhood obstacle, I am blindsided by another. I become frustrated with the dormant messages I socially learned throughout my childhood.

In my most vulnerable stages of existence, an inactive message becomes resurrected. For instance, my new confession is I do not like to be told no. After I have envisioned a plan, decided on how I will strategize to accomplish the plan, I then proceed with seeking an agreement from others that the plan may affect or those I would like to be a part of the plan.

When the answer is no – something takes place in the pit of my stomach. I quickly reply, "Oh, ok. No problem", while I feel rejected. After I have created the plan in my head, I set my goal for target. The truth is, when the plan is not achieved I believe I have failed. Feeling like a failure is the worst pain anyone can inflict onto self. The feelings of failure then causes me to feel lost and out of control, prone to manipulate, and insecure about the next steps. You have just witnessed a voice attack! To confront a voice attack you must first identify the attack. Dr. Robert Firestone, a clinical psychologist and the author of *Voice therapy: A psychotherapeutic approach to self-destructive behavior*, suggested voice therapy to combat negative thought patterns. Once the thought pattern has been identified as negative – for example, I use to think *"By the time I get married, I may have complications with pregnancy"* – I had to identify where the thought originated from and why the origination has such an influence on my behavior. The thought of my new revelation angst's me. The expectation of never being told 'no' sounded childish. As a kid, the indirect and direct messages I heard from my parents, teachers, and caretakers were "If you do what is right, you can have what you want", "Bring home good grades and you will be rewarded." These messages created a do-gooder mentality in me and possibly a little self-absorption.

According to my plan, I should have been married. Since I am not married, I believed I failed in my relationship with Charlie.

I was determined to wait for his perception of me to change due to our tumultuous past and get him to marry me. Since none of the above worked (because Charlie use to tell me yes) I believed any new relationship on the horizon might be sabotaged by me and my expectations. The memory of watching how my mother responded to unmet expectations within her relationships gripped me. I am her seed; I have perpetrated the same behaviors with Charlie. In the third step of voice therapy, Dr. Firestone suggested developing a plan of action to counteract the voice.

For me, I would have to acknowledge that I am not my mother. Secondly, I would have to admit that though I perceive to have followed a plan that works for me, my plan is in constant formation; however, everyone has a plan, which might not align with mine. That is okay, the world will not truly end. I do at times, experience conflicted thoughts about my marital status. But as I continue to become aware and confront my unhealthy messages through staying in touch with reality, I am comforted that I am not married and making someone else's life miserable because I am still learning to do what is right by me first; well, by God first. This truth definitely allows me to live freely and gives others the permission to do the same.

GROOMED to Bloom

I was created in God's image; for God's purpose; created in God's likeness that I may be a bird soaring throughout the land.
I am man but in spirit I am God's masterpiece.
God still created me. Yes, complicated in all of my ways, For God's purpose God receives glory when I am refined into God's workmanship that has marked lives with my unique expression.
God has made no one like me and I am like no one.
I take all that I am, all that I am yet to be and continue on my journey.
I was created to **BLOOM**.

References

[1]Brown, L. M., & Gilligan, C. (1993). Meeting at the crossroads: Women's psychology and girls' development. *Feminism & Psychology, 3,* 11-35.

[2]Burrow-Sanchez, J. J. (2006). Understanding adolescent substance abuse: Prevalence, risk factors, and clinical implications. *Journal of Counseling & Development, 84,* 283-290.

Chapman, G. (2009). *The five love languages.* Chicago, IL: Northfield Publishing.

[4]Cole, E. L. (1987). *Communication, sex, and money.* Wheaton, IL: Tyndale House Publishers, Inc.

Firestone, R. W. (1988). *Voice therapy: A psychotherapeutic approach to self-destructive behavior.* New York, NY: Human Sciences Press.

[6]Gilligan, C. (1996). The centrality of relationship in human development: A puzzle, some evidence, and a theory. In G. G. Noam & K. W. Fischer (Eds.), *Development and vulnerability in close relationships,* (p237-261). Mahwah, NJ: Erlbaum.

Hammond, M. M., & Brooks, J. A. (2009). *The unspoken rules of love: What women don't know and men don't tell.* Colorado Springs, CO: Water Brook Press.

Fuller, L. B. (2012). The impact of structured group counseling on resiliency, self-efficacy, and racial identity among African American female teenagers. PsycINFO, *Dissertation Abstracts International Section A: Humanities and Social Sciences, 73,* (5-A), 0419-4209.

[9]James, W. (1909). *The meaning of truth, A sequel to 'pragmatism'.* New York, NY: Longmans, Green, and Company.

[10]Gilligan, C. (2008). Exit-voice dilemmas in adolescent development. In D. L. Browning (Ed.), *Adolescent identities: A collection of readings,* (p141-156). New York, NY: Analytic Press.

[11]Gilligan, C. (1977). In a different voice: Women's conception of self and of morality. *Harvard Educational Review, 47,* 481-517.

[12]Gilligan, C. (1991). Women's psychological development: Implications for psychotherapy. In C. Gilligan, A. Rogers, & D. Tolman (Eds.), *Women, girls, and psychotherapy: Reframing resistance.* Binghamton, NY: Haworth Press.

ABOUT THE AUTHOR

Since a teenager, Dr. LaShonda B. Fuller has used Writing as an avenue to share her experiences. Her passion for communication influenced her pursuit of a Bachelors degree in Journalism at Bowling Green State University, where she also pursued a Masters degree in Guidance and Counseling. Her love for wanting to help people heal from emotional wounds encouraged Dr. LaShonda to further her education in Counselor Education at Western Michigan University. Dr. LaShonda is intentional about bridging her two obsessions to impact the world around her and therefore, blogs to keep her readers informed and motivated to ACT!

www.tutenterprises.org

www.ingramcontent.com/pod-product-compliance
Lightning Source LLC
Chambersburg PA
CBHW021004090426
42738CB00007B/647